THE LAST GREAT
Anointing

MORRIS CERULLO

FOREWORD BY C. PETER WAGNER

Renew

A Division of Gospel Light
Ventura, California, U.S.A.

Published by Renew Books
A Division of Gospel Light
Ventura, California, U.S.A.
Printed in U.S.A.

Renew Books is a ministry of Gospel Light, an evangelical Christian publisher dedicated to serving the local church. We believe God's vision for Gospel Light is to provide church leaders with biblical, user-friendly materials that will help them evangelize, disciple and minister to children, youth and families.

It is our prayer that this Renew book will help you discover biblical truth for your own life and help you meet the needs of others. May God richly bless you.

For a free catalog of resources from Renew Books/Gospel Light please contact your Christian supplier or contact us at 1-800-4-GOSPEL or at www.gospellight.com.

Cover Design by Kevin Keller
Interior Design by Rob Williams

LIBRARY OF CONGRESS CATALOGING-IN-PUBLICATION DATA
Cerullo, Morris.
    The last great anointing / Morris Cerullo
        p.   cm.
    ISBN 0-8307-2472-9 (trade paper)
    1. Prophecy—Christianity. 2. Prayer. 3. Eschatology. 4. Great
Commission (Bible). 5. Evangelistic work. I. Title.
    BR115.P8C47   1999   99-20264
    243—dc21   CIP

1 2 3 4 5 6 7 8 9 10 11 12 13 14 15 / 05 04 03 02 01 00 99

Rights for publishing this book in other languages are contracted by Gospel Literature International (GLINT). GLINT also provides technical help for the adaptation, translation and publishing of Bible study resources and books in scores of languages worldwide. For further information, contact GLINT, P.O. Box 4060, Ontario, CA 91761-1003, U.S.A. You may also send E-mail to Glintint@aol.com or visit their website at www.glint.org.

CONTENTS

FOREWORD

As I first read the manuscript of this book, the Lord flashed into my mind an incident in 1989 in which I received what at that time was undoubtedly the clearest and most direct prophetic word I had yet experienced. He said, "My son, speak it out: tell the world that 1990 will truly be a hinge year!" I obeyed and spoke it to the best of my ability in a short article in *Ministries Today* magazine.

The decade of the 1990s is now nearing its end, and there is no question at all that it was truly what the Spirit was saying to the churches. I, of course, was not the only one who was hearing from God at this time. Many others were also hearing from God, including my good friend, Morris Cerullo. I want to explain why I believe that Brother Cerullo's book, *The Last Great Anointing*, can be regarded as one of the Kingdom capstones of this decade. .

Of the many things that God has been showing the Church over the past few years, the two at the top of His agenda, in my opinion, are powerful prayer and the completion of the Great Commission, and how the two are intimately and inextricably interrelated. The Body of Christ has long believed in prayer and in world evangelization, but we have been taken by the Holy Spirit to new and unprecedented levels in both.

Largely because we have been learning how prayer can be truly *powerful* prayer, our generation is the first generation since the time of Christ that literally has the potential of completing the Great Commission. In fact, no past generation could even measure the remaining task with any sort of precision, but we can. And it is happening! For example, of 1,739 significantly large unreached people groups at the beginning of the decade, only around 500 have yet to see an initial church planting movement among them. That fact alone far surpasses anything that could have been reported in the past.

Why is this happening? God has raised up the most massive worldwide prayer movement that anyone could have imagined, and it is gaining strength daily. There are no heroic figures in this movement—it is the rising of the saints of God. The global prayer movement is truly out of control! A few of us have been trying to keep up as much as we can, and to help coordinate segments of the movement here and there.

Among these is Morris Cerullo, who is believing God for a Global Prayer Strike Force of 10 million intercessors as a prayer covering for the massive Mission to All the World.

The Body of Christ has moved rapidly from level to level in prayer for the lost souls of the world over the past few years. We are doing things now, almost as a matter of routine, that we did not even have words for 10 years ago. But we are not through! Brother Cerullo believes, and I agree, that God is about to move us into a dimension of authority in our prayers that will require us to coin even newer words to describe the new things that the Holy Spirit will be doing through His people. Brother Cerullo says, "We must now go deep into the realm of the Spirit, to not only bind the power of the enemy, but to completely destroy his strongholds."

I was struck as I read this word from the Lord through Brother Cerullo: "This prophetic prayer anointing will not be released upon everyone. There will be Christians who will be unwilling or afraid to let go of their preconceived ideas, man-made traditions and doctrines, to step into the fresh flow of God's Spirit. They will cling to the past and rely upon their limited understanding instead of abandoning themselves in full surrender to the direction and anointing of the Holy Spirit." I, for one, do not want to be found in that number!

I have kept close track of the literature on prayer that has been released for the mobilization of the Body of Christ in this decade. What an awesome unfolding of the plan of God, taking us from glory to glory and from strength to strength! These books, some of which I have written, have reported, they have explained, they have analyzed, they have motivated, they have laid theological foundations, and they have excited believers everywhere.

But the book you are about to read is different. The reason I have labeled it as one of the Kingdom capstones of our time is that this book, perhaps more than any other, will *impart*. It will impart to you, as it did to me, a fresh anointing of God, not just for prayer in general, but for powerful, strategic-level warfare prayer to tear down the strongholds that the enemy has been using to keep masses of people in spiritual darkness for ages.

The completion of the Great Commission and the coming of Jesus our King has never been nearer. When it comes, I want to be one who has received God's "final anointing" to be on the front lines, and I know that you do too! This book can go a long way toward making it happen!

C. Peter Wagner
World Prayer Center of Colorado Springs

INTRODUCTION

Beloved, this is not just another book on prayer. There are thousands of good books on prayer by anointed men and women of God on the bookshelves of Christian stores today. This is not a book on the methodology of prayer.

It is a prophetic book with the revelation God gave me regarding what I believe is the last great anointing God is now releasing upon the Church before Christ returns. Forget the religious traditional approach to prayer. God wants to bring you into a completely new dimension of prayer where you totally abandon yourself and yield to His Spirit 100 percent!

In 1995 God spoke to me and gave me this prophecy for the Body of Christ:

> *God is going to take us into the spirit world, into a new strategic level of warfare prayer. When you receive this revelation, there will not be any power of the enemy that will be able to stand before what God will put in your spirit and your life!*
>
> *You will never be defeated in your prayers again!*

You will demolish strongholds in your family, in your home, in your community and in your nation.

This does not mean you will be free from problems or that every prayer you pray will always be answered in the manner you desire. There are many Christians who do not know how to pray and they have never developed a strong prayer life. When you enter into this experience, your prayer life will never be the same. You will experience victory after victory and a new intimacy with God.

I have written this book under a heavy prophetic anointing. It is my desire that as you read, you too will experience a prophetic mantle of intercession coming over your life.

More than 40 years ago God revealed to me in a vision the great end-time outpouring of His Spirit that He will release before Christ returns. What I saw and experienced in that vision is just as real to me today as it was 40 years ago!

It was an awesome experience for me as a young 26-year-old evangelist. It was in 1957, in Lima, Ohio. I was conducting a crusade and staying in a little room in the YMCA. It was early one morning before dawn. The shades were drawn and the room was dark. Suddenly the room was flooded with a supernatural light. Immediately I fell on my face and prostrated myself before the Lord.

As I lay there, a vision began to appear. Stretched before me was a massive multitude, too great to number. It is hard to describe, but it was a large place and it seemed as if I could see the actual curvature of the earth.

The great multitude was standing under a cloud-filled sky. As I looked up into those clouds there was an expectation and excitement because I sensed something was going to appear. As I gazed into the clouds, raindrops began to fall from the heavens.

It was not a natural rain—it was supernatural. There were giant drops of rain coming down with great deliberateness.

As the raindrops fell upon the people, their substance was more like oil than water. Rather than splashing like rain, the giant drops seemed to flow over the multitude.

"Lord, what does this rain mean?" I cried out.

Then, out of the light a voice spoke. *This rain is the outpouring of My Holy Spirit.*

I then realized what I was seeing was the outpouring of the Holy Spirit upon the multitude. My first thought was to try to determine to which denomination or group this multitude belonged. The more I looked, the more I realized there was no denominational distinction.

The question upon my heart was, "Lord, in the past You have brought Your revelation through a particular group."

There was no answer.

I thought to myself, *If I cannot see the group, then surely I will see the man God has chosen as an instrument to lead this new outpouring of the Holy Spirit.* I thought of the prominent men whom God was using in that hour, and my eyes searched and searched through the multitude to find one of them, but I could not distinguish anyone in the multitude.

"Lord, are you trying to show me that You are choosing me to lead this new outpouring of Your Spirit?" I asked.

God spoke to me in that tiny room. It was impossible to tell from which direction His voice came because the sound of His voice seemed to fill the entire room.

God said to me, "Son, you don't see the group or the man because there will not be anyone leading this revival. What I am about to do on the earth will be entirely without human direction, so that no man can put his name on it. This will not be the work of a man, but of the Holy Spirit."

There is one factor that distinguishes this outpouring of the Holy Spirit from the rest: It will be the last great move of the Holy Spirit upon mankind. Its purpose is not simply to revive, renew or restore. Its purpose is to make ready a people prepared to meet the Lord!

God revealed to me that He is releasing this last great anointing to enable the Church to fulfill the Great Commission and bring in the greatest harvest of souls in the history of the Church.

God has revealed that He will bring us into a new dimension of authority in our prayers where our words, spoken with authority, invested in the promises of God, will enable us to confront every stronghold of the enemy!

In the 52 years of my ministry to the nations of the world, God has taken me onto the front lines of battle in prayer. And He has now released me to share key truths and prophetic revelations that I believe He will use to release an end-time prophetic prayer anointing upon your life.

Morris Cerullo

C H A P T E R

1

AN END-TIME PROPHETIC PRAYER ANOINTING!

The entire world is reeling under political and economic crises. Earthquakes, floods, hurricanes, famines and other natural disasters are bringing widespread devastation and death. At this time God is releasing what I believe is the last great anointing upon His Church.

We are people of God's destiny, called and anointed by God, privileged to be alive in this end-time hour in which Jesus will return in all His power and glory! We are living in a unique period of time, unlike any other in the history of the Church. It is a time of great excitement and rejoicing for God's people.

Jesus is coming!

This is undoubtedly the greatest hour for the Church. I am sitting on the edge of my seat, waiting, looking and longing for the day when the skies will roll back and Christ will return in all His power and glory for His Church.

It is also a time of great spiritual intensity. We are facing spiritual challenges no other generation has ever faced. We are involved in a fierce end-time battle for the millions of souls who have still never heard the gospel! A fierce battle is raging. The nations of the world are the battlegrounds where we are waging a relentless war for souls who are facing an eternity in hell, without God.

Satan, knowing he has a very short time, is pouring out his fury upon the Church. Christians are facing the greatest satanic attacks they have ever experienced. Simultaneously, as Satan is launching a frontal attack against the Church to slow down the progress we have been making in taking nations for the kingdom of God, God is pouring out a powerful, prophetic end-time anointing upon His people.

One of the major keys to being on the forefront of what God is doing and receiving all that He has planned for you to experience in this end-time hour is *spiritual sensitivity.* God wants you to be spiritually alert at all times. He wants your spiritual eyes and ears ready to discern the things of the Spirit and clearly understand what He is doing, what He is saying and what He is directing you to do. Your spiritual focus must be set!

God wants you to know what the Holy Spirit is saying in this critical hour before Christ returns. Don't look to man; don't look to your own limited understanding; don't look to denominations or organizations. Look to the Holy Spirit to get a fresh word from God Almighty! Knowing what God is doing, His purpose and plan and His timing will make the difference between walking in His power and anointing or living in confusion and defeat.

GOD SENDS ANOINTINGS TO ACCOMPLISH SPECIFIC PURPOSES

You need to recognize and understand the different anointings from God and know His purposes. *An anointing is a specific, divine enablement given by God to an individual or group to accomplish a specific task.*

Throughout the history of the Church we have seen God release special anointings to fulfill specific purposes. In 1964, God spoke to me and said, "Son, I am going to send a new anointing of My divine healing power to America." I prayed and waited upon God to reveal to me the key to the release of this new anointing. It wasn't until eight years later, in 1972, that God revealed the key to this new anointing He promised to send to America. He revealed it to me in the strangest place and under the most unusual circumstances.

I was scheduled to conduct a crusade in India—one that I waited for with the greatest apprehension. My oldest son, David, went to India with our technician to do the set-up work for the crusade. He met me at the airport when I arrived and I will never forget the look on his face. When I first saw him, I thought I was seeing a ghost. I asked him, "David, what's wrong?"

He said, "Dad, I don't know. There is something in the air—something in the atmosphere of this nation. I have been with you in South America, in Europe and in other places, but there is something here that makes me sick. I do not understand it."

I knew what David felt. I had been in India before. I knew the Indian people worshiped 330 million false gods. The oppression of those demon spirits is so heavy you can feel it in the air.

I went immediately to my room and began to pray. Something came over me during this prayer that I had never felt before. I had prayed in all of our crusades many hours each day, but something in my inner being felt as if it were literally being torn apart.

I began to travail and call out certain things by name. In the name of Jesus, I began to bind the powers of the enemy—the spirits of sin, sickness, false religion, cults, idolatry and the false prophets of Baal. I found myself binding the power of Satan that controlled the religious leaders who might use their influence to try to destroy the crusade. In the Spirit I was binding these powers of darkness, not really understanding what I was doing. In that prayer I loosed the spirit of salvation and the spirit of healing.

When I went out to the meeting, the battle was already won! The spirit of salvation was upon those people, and all I had to do was preach a simple gospel message and they were willing to receive Jesus Christ as their personal Lord and Savior. Something happened during my time of prayer that released the miracle power of God! The power of darkness that was oppressing and controlling the people was bound! Salvation and healing were loosed!

We went through the whole campaign in India without one problem. On about the fourth day of the crusade, God spoke to me and said, "Son, can you see it? Can you see that as soon as you begin to use the same keys to victory in North America that you are using here, the sooner you will see the same anointing in North America?"

It was like my entire being was illuminated, glowing with the light of the Holy Spirit. There in India, I realized there was no difference between the battles on foreign fields and the battles in North America. The same key to victory that shook countries overseas would bring the victory in America. I realized that spiritual warfare was the same everywhere.

In 1975, I began to teach and share with all my partners this powerful revelation God gave me on spiritual warfare. This revelation showed me how to go deep into the spirit realm to locate the enemy, and how to bind evil spirits and loose spirits of salvation, healing and deliverance in Jesus' name. As a result of this revelation on the new anointing God gave me, we began to receive more testimonies and reports of answered prayer than we had ever received in the history of my ministry!

GOD IS TAKING US TO A NEW POSITION OF POWER AND AUTHORITY IN PRAYER

Now, as this new end-time prophetic prayer anointing is being released, God is taking us higher into a new dimension of power and authority in prayer. We must go deep into the realm of the Spirit, not only to bind the power of the enemy, but to completely destroy his strongholds.

Jesus gave us these powerful keys of binding and loosing. He said,

> "Whatsoever ye shall bind on earth shall be bound in heaven: and whatsoever ye shall loose on earth shall be loosed in heaven. Again I say unto you, That if two of you shall agree on earth as touching any thing that they shall ask, *it shall be done for them of my Father which is in heaven.* For where two or three are gathered together in my name, there am I in the midst of them" (Matt. 18:18-20, emphasis added).

In prayer as you begin to travail, to wrestle, and to penetrate deep into the spirit realm, God will begin to reveal to you the spirits, the powers, and the root causes of the battle you are facing. Your battle is not against any sickness such as arthritis, diabetes, heart disease, hearing loss or any other disorder that the enemy has put upon your body. Your battle is not with your husband, wife, child or any other family member. Your battle is not with a boss or fellow employee. Your battle is not with your financial condition, your lack of finances and overdue bills.

We are not waging a natural war and we are not using natural weapons. The apostle Paul said,

> For we wrestle not against flesh and blood, but against
> principalities, against powers, against the rulers of the
> darkness of this world, against spiritual wickedness in
> high places (Eph. 6:12).

Your warfare is not on the surface. It is not in the circumstances as you see them. Your warfare is not in the natural world
that is governed by your five natural senses. Your battle is in the
spirit realm. Behind the circumstances you are facing there are
spiritual powers and rulers of darkness at work. These powers
are behind political struggles; these principalities are behind
Communism, Hinduism, Islam, Shintoism, Buddhism, Ani-
mism, Taoism, Confucianism and Spiritism. They are behind
racial prejudice, crime, violence and unjust economic conditions.
Nations of the earth, there are evil forces at work, and the same
is true in your family struggles and personal struggles.

There are spirits of confusion, fear, frustration, promiscuity,
homosexuality, lust, envy, jealousy, hatred, violence, rebellion,
murder, suicide, resentment, selfishness and many others that
have been released in the world today and are working to kill and
destroy.

Before you can tear down the strongholds the enemy has built
in your home, city and nation, you must first locate the enemy—
the spiritual forces that are the root cause of the circumstances.
The only possible way of locating these spiritual forces that are
the *root cause* of the battles you are facing is through deep, intercessory prayer. Without it, you are like a blindfolded soldier. You
won't be able to recognize the enemy and you won't be able to
use your powerful weapons of warfare to defeat him.

> For the weapons of our warfare are not physical [weapons
> of flesh and blood], but they are mighty before God for

the overthrow and destruction of strongholds (2 Cor. 10:4, *AMP.*).

In Madras, India, I had fought and penetrated the barriers built by evil forces. After I had bound the evil spirits, I loosed the ministering spirits in prayer which God had revealed to me and then I was able to go out on the platform and claim the victories. The very first night of the meeting, 50,000 Hindus received Jesus Christ as their Lord and Savior. This great victory was won in prayer!

We must be careful not to limit this power and authority to a formula or to mere words that we speak. It is not a superficial thing where a person is simply speaking words. It is not something that is based on emotion. Binding and loosing is a mighty spiritual weapon that must be used in the spirit realm in prayer and on your face before God!

A person can scream and shout all day, "I bind you, Satan!" but Satan will just laugh at him, unless the binding and loosing has been done *in the Spirit!* The battle must *first* be won on your face before God through weeping, travailing, interceding and battling these evil spirits through the mighty weapon of prayer.

YOU ARE THE VICTOR! YOU ARE THE AGGRESSOR!

You must remember, we are not simply talking about words coming out of our mouths. Our prayers must be Holy Spirit energized and spoken with God's power and authority. The battle must first be won in the Spirit and in prayer!

The apostle Paul told the Ephesians:

In conclusion, be strong in the Lord [be empowered through your union with Him]; draw your strength from Him [that strength which His boundless might provides].

Put on God's whole armor [the armor of a heavy-armed soldier which God supplies], that you may be able successfully to stand up against [all] the strategies and deceits of the devil. For we are not wrestling with flesh and blood [contending only with physical opponents], but against the despotisms, against the powers, against [the master spirits who are] the world rulers of this present darkness, against the spirit forces of wickedness in the heavenly (supernatural) sphere (Eph. 6:10-12, *AMP.*).

By His Spirit God has equipped you to stand *successfully* against all the strategies of the devil. You are the victor! Through the anointing of His Spirit, He has divinely enabled you to face and defeat all the evil powers and principalities working on the earth today!

After listing various pieces of the spiritual armor God has given us, Paul completes the list by including the powerful weapon of prayer. In Ephesians 6:18 *(AMP.)*, Paul said:

Pray at all times (on every occasion, in every season) in the Spirit, with all [manner of] prayer and entreaty. To that end keep alert and watch with strong purpose and perseverance, interceding in behalf of all the saints (God's consecrated people).

Having first won the battle in prayer, you will be able to simply speak the word of healing as Jesus did. When you see those who are blind, deaf and crippled, you will not need to *ask* God to heal them; you will be able to speak with authority, "See! Hear! Walk! Be healed in the name of Jesus and it will be done!"

You will not hesitate or wonder if the work will be done. You will be able to face every need, every sickness and every disease knowing that Christ is living *in you* and that He is doing the works of God through you. You will be able to face the problems in your life, in your family relationships, in your finances and on your job without fear or worry. You will be able to claim victories in every area of your life, knowing the work has been done and the enemy has been bound and cast out in prayer.

WE WILL SEE AN AWESOME MANIFESTATION OF GOD'S POWER

In 1989, on my way back from Perth, Australia, God gave me a revelation regarding five major crises and five major waves of the Holy Spirit coming in the decade of the nineties. God showed me that the '90s would be God's "Decade of Destiny and the Decade of the Holy Spirit." He revealed to me that He was going to release an awesome manifestation of His power on the Church that would result in the greatest harvest of souls in the history of the Church.

In October of 1994, the Father spoke to me again and gave me an awesome revelation. God said: "Son, you're going to see more souls won into My kingdom in the next six years than in all the history of Christianity put together."

Something beyond what you and I have ever dreamed is going to happen in the spiritual realm in the next few years that will break through the current structure of the Church, to break us out of the "ruts of the field" and empower us to get the job done! A vital part of this new move of God will be an incredible wave of intercession. As the intercession of God's people rises to heaven, God will begin to release the floodgates of heaven!

There will be an acceleration and multiplication taking place within the Body of Christ that will supersede anything that we have experienced. God will supernaturally empower and equip us to reach the world with the gospel and reap a greater harvest of souls in this decade than at any other time in the history of the Church!

AN ENERGIZING GLOBAL CALL TO PRAYER!
At the beginning of 1995, God began to show me how He would release a new powerful prayer anointing upon the Church!

The purpose of this anointing is not so that Christians can simply enjoy the blessings of God (shout, rejoice, laugh, dance in the Spirit). The purpose of this last great anointing is to divinely enable the Church to fulfill God's purposes and bring in the great end-time harvest before Christ returns, and to penetrate the last satanic strongholds over closed nations.

After 52 years of ministry, and walking very closely with the Lord, I am convinced that there is now a new anointing rising up. It is an energizing, global call to prayer that is coming upon the people of God. As a result of this powerful anointing that is coming upon true believers, we will see the end-time gathering of the greatest harvest this world has ever known!

As sure as I am alive, I believe we will have to pray King Jesus back! There are many doors that are still closed to the gospel and will swing open only if something supernatural occurs. The Islamic, Buddhist, Hindu and other major strongholds of the enemy can only be penetrated and torn down as God's people enter into this new dimension of spiritual warfare prayer.

GOD IS GOING TO HAVE A PEOPLE!

More than 40 years ago, I was just a young man in my early 20s when God visited me and said to me:

Son, there is coming a day when I am going to draw a line between so-called sideline compromisers. No longer will My

Church be able to have one foot in the world and the other foot in My presence. I will not tolerate it in the end-time.

He spoke this to me 40 years ago, and I believe that day is here now. Receive this prophetic word into your spirit right now!

God is going to have a people in this end-time hour! His hand will be strong upon them. His glory will cover them. They will operate on a new level and new spiritual dimension of prayer that will enable them to supersede every natural limitation. God's anointing will be so strong upon them they will be living witnesses to the world that Jesus is Who He claims to be—the Son of the living God!

God is preparing Himself a people! He is working inside them. Something is happening inside their beings. They are dying to everything of the flesh. They are dying to everything of self. They are dying to every ambition. They are coming to the place where the only thing that matters in this world is their life with God and how God can use them. Can you sense this happening inside you?

I believe this end-time anointing God is now releasing is the last great anointing before Christ returns. This anointing is unique. It will release the greatest manifestation of signs and wonders and miracles this world has ever known. It is an awesome prayer anointing that is coming upon the Church to bring us into a new strategic level of spiritual warfare prayer. And the greatest result will be an unfolding of the revelation of who Jesus really is.

There is no way, in the natural, to penetrate the 10/40 Window of two billion lost souls and reap the harvest. We cannot do it based upon our limited natural understanding. It is a spiritual battle that must be fought and won in the Spirit through a new strategic level of warfare prayer!

We will not be able to penetrate the strongholds of the enemy, tear them down in Jesus' name and reap the great end-time harvest of souls at our current level of spiritual experience. The great majority of Christians sitting in our churches today have a very limited understanding of the true power of prayer God intends the Church to have.

There are many who have "head knowledge" concerning spiritual warfare, but they haven't entered into an *experience* where they know how to wage war in the heavenlies on behalf of their families, cities and nations.

The Victory Belongs to You, but You Must Declare It!

Although we are seeing the greatest prayer movement in the history of the Church and millions mobilizing for prayer, there is only a small minority who truly understand the position God wants them to take in prayer to affect changes and fulfill God's plan and purposes in their homes, churches, cities and nations.

Already I can sense God stirring something deep inside His people. God is saying to you:

I am preparing you. The consummation of the ages is here. I have chosen you for this hour. I am positioning you for the end-time battle. The harvest of the earth is ready, but you must go forth into battle in My power and authority, to wrest the souls of men, women and children out of Satan's hands.

Awake, My people! Rise up! Put on your battle gear. Array yourselves in My power and strength. The battle belongs to you, but you must declare it! You must pursue it with all diligence and perseverance. Do not withhold anything. Lay aside every distraction, every weight and every encumbrance. I am the Lord your God who leads you into battle.

Keep your heart and mind fixed upon Me! Sharpen your spiritual senses. Wait before Me. Set yourselves to hear My voice and to follow My leading. As you wait before Me, I will reveal My plan and strategy for this hour. Do not rely on past victories or lean on your own understanding. There is no hour like this hour! Only those who truly know Me and hear My voice will understand and know the battle plan for this end-time hour.

The time has come for My people to win the greatest battle of all the ages. But you must prepare yourselves by waiting before Me. This is your strength.

As you know Me in My fullness, you will hear My voice. As I reveal Myself to you, you will not be fearful nor waver in doubt. Your steps will be ordered by Me. They will be made clear and My power will flow through you. You will not stumble or fall but will march forward to defeat the work of the enemy.

You are the victor! You are the aggressor! The power I am releasing within you assures you that you will not be defeated. You will overcome even as I have overcome!

Receive this prophetic word of the Lord into your spirit!

RAISE UP A PRAYER COVERING OVER THE WORLD!

When God spoke to me in August 1996 and revealed the Mission to All the World mandate of reaching the world with the gospel by the end of the year 2000, He also showed me the major key to its fulfillment. God told me: *Raise up a prayer covering over the world.*

He gave me a very specific directive. He showed me that now is the time for His Church to begin to pray for Christ to return. Before Christ comes, a mighty cry must rise up and cover the earth. The prayer on the lips of every born-again believer must be, "Come, Lord Jesus!" Deep from within the innermost recesses of our spirits, there must be a cry, a yearning after and a longing for His return.

God's end-time plan will be fulfilled as the Church begins to pray! The Mission to All the World will be accomplished as we raise up a prayer covering over the world!

A prayer covering is a spiritual shield that is raised by prayer, that surrounds you, your family, unsaved loved ones, your home, your pastor and your church. In placing this prayer covering over the world, we are completely wrapping the entire world and surrounding it with prayer. As millions of Christians join together to raise up this prayer covering, the darkness of the world will be pierced, and we will see the greatest manifestation of God's power released in the history of the world!

This prayer covering over the world will *open the windows of heaven and release the supernatural power of God!* With all my spirit, soul and body, I am convinced that the only way we will be able to fulfill the Mission to All the World mandate is through *united, concentrated, strategic warfare prayer!*

When I refer to "united" prayer, I am not speaking about Christians and churches just coming together for corporate prayer meetings. United prayer involves being joined together with one mind, one heart and one purpose with God's will and plan.

IT'S TIME TO GET SPIRITUALLY FOCUSED!

One of the reasons the Early Church experienced powerful breakthroughs when they prayed is because they were united together with *one accord* and were focused on the calling and commission Christ had given them. He told them,

"All power is given unto me in heaven and in earth. Go ye therefore, and teach all nations, baptizing them in the Name of the Father, and of the Son, and of the Holy Ghost" (Matt. 28:18,19).

[The disciples] all continued with one accord in prayer and supplication. And when the day of Pentecost was fully come, they were all with one accord in one place. And the multitude of them that believed were of one heart and of one soul (Acts 1:14; 2:1; 4:32).

After Peter and John were released from prison, beaten and commanded not to speak or preach in Jesus' name, they did not retreat. They did not call a meeting to discuss and plan their strategy based on their own natural understanding. They prayed! They had a Holy Ghost prayer meeting and they lifted up their voices to God with one accord. Listen to their prayer:

"Sovereign Lord," they said, "you made the heaven and the earth and the sea, and everything in them. You spoke by the Holy Spirit through the mouth of your servant, our father David: 'Why do the nations rage and the peoples plot in vain? The kings of the earth take their stand and the rulers gather together against the Lord and against his anointed One.' Indeed Herod and Pontius Pilate met together with Gentiles and the people of Israel in this city to conspire against your holy servant Jesus, whom you anointed. They did what your power and will had decided beforehand should happen. Now, Lord, consider their threats and enable your servants to speak your word with great boldness" (Acts 4:24-28, *NIV*).

They did not ask God to stop the persecution. They prayed for the power and boldness to proclaim the gospel in the face of persecution and death, with signs and wonders manifested in the name of Jesus.

"And now, Lord, behold their threatenings: and grant unto thy servants, that with all boldness they may speak thy word. By stretching forth thine hand to heal; and that signs and wonders may be done by the name of thy holy child Jesus." And when they had prayed, the place was shaken where they were assembled together; and they were all filled with the Holy Ghost, and they spake the word of God with boldness (Acts 4:29-31).

When they finished praying, the place where they were meeting shook under the mighty hand of God! God heard and answered their prayer. The result of their prayer was evident!

And they continued to speak the Word of God with freedom and boldness and courage. And with great strength and ability and power the apostles delivered their testimony to the resurrection of the Lord Jesus, and great grace (loving-kindness and favor and goodwill) rested richly upon them all (Acts 4:31,33, *AMP.*).

The Scriptures also tell us:

By the hands of the apostles were many signs and wonders wrought among the people (Acts 5:12).

Beloved, the Church of Jesus Christ needs to get back to the basics! We need to get into the presence of almighty God and pray with one mind and one accord until we receive the same holy boldness and anointing. We need to pray this same prayer and ask God to manifest His miracle-working power through us in the power and authority of Jesus' name as a mighty witness to the world that He is who He claims to be—the Son of the living God!

 It's time to seek God's face until we hear from heaven and our lives are on fire with the power of the Holy Spirit!

The world is waiting for the reality of the gospel to be demonstrated by the Church!

We preach salvation, healing and deliverance in Jesus' name. As His delegated authority upon this earth, we must come into an experience where His power is manifested through us to proclaim the gospel to heal the sick, cast out devils and establish His kingdom in the nations of the world.

CHURCH, IT'S TIME TO PRAY!

It's time to seek God's face until we hear from heaven and our lives are set on fire with the power of the Holy Spirit!

Jesus said, "Is it not written, My house shall be called of all nations the house of prayer?" (Mark 11:17). This is the true purpose of the Church. And as God is releasing this prophetic prayer anointing, He is bringing us back to this original purpose. Receive this prophecy into your spirit!

As the Body of Christ responds to this end-time call to prayer, God's power will be poured out in an awesome demonstration,

greater than anything the Church has ever known or experienced,
to destroy these remaining strongholds and bring in the greatest
harvest of souls in the history of the Church!

Repeating prayers based on "head knowledge" or following a
"formula" for prayer does not produce results. There are many
Christians who are praying prayers, but they are devoid of power.
They are saying all the right things. They try to bind the power
of the enemy. They try to take authority over evil powers and
principalities and try to command Satan to loose his hold. Yet,
the power of God is not being manifested. Their prayers are just
mere words—sincere, but lifeless—without any real power!

There are Christians who are praying what appear to be
high-powered prayers, but there is nothing behind the prayers.
The emotions are stirred, there is a lot of noise, but the spiritual
results are missing.

Are you ready for God to release this anointing on you, taking
you into this new strategic level of warfare prayer?

WE ARE ENFORCERS!

The major distinguishing factor of this last great anointing will
be a new level of *spiritual authority*. God is going to bring us into
a new dimension of authority in our prayers where our very
words, spoken with authority, invested in the promises of God,
will enable us to confront every stronghold of the enemy!

When we talk about authority, we're not talking about merely
saying words. We're not talking about speaking the Word only. Our
words are spoken with authority and invested in the promises of
God!

God's people must have a new understanding of prayer. I
like what Paul Billheimer wrote in his book, *Destined for the
Throne.*

Prayer is not begging God to do something which He is unwilling to do. It is not overcoming reluctance in God. Prayer is enforcing the victory that Christ won over Satan! It is implementing upon earth, heaven's decisions concerning the affairs of men. Calvary legally destroyed Satan and cancelled all of his claims.

God placed the enforcement of Calvary's victory in the hands of the Church. It is our job to see to it that the victory Jesus won is enforced on this earth!

> *The type of spiritual authority God plans for the Church to operate in is nothing less than the same power and authority Christ demonstrated!*

The authority God intends the Church to have, and the authority we must have to take the nations of this world for the kingdom of God through our prayers is not a natural authority. It is a divine, God-given, Holy Ghost imparted authority! The type of spiritual authority God plans for the Church to operate in is nothing less than the *same* power and authority Christ demonstrated!

Jesus came to earth to destroy the works of the devil. "For this purpose the Son of God was manifested, that he might destroy the works of the devil" (1 John 3:8). He faced and defeated Satan not in His own authority, but in the power and authority of His Father's name. He said, "I have not come on My own authority and of My own accord. I have come in My Father's name" (John 7:28; 5:43, *AMP.*).

Jesus was called, commissioned, sent to this earth and anointed to fulfill God's plan and purpose. While Jesus did not cease being God, He humbled Himself and lived on earth as a man. Christ the Creator, all-powerful, all knowing, and everywhere present God stripped Himself. He voluntarily and unselfishly laid aside His divine attributes (see Phil. 2:5-7).

When the appointed time came for Jesus to begin His ministry, He came to the Jordan River where He was baptized and anointed with the Holy Spirit.

> God anointed and consecrated Jesus of Nazareth with the [Holy] Spirit and with strength and ability and power; how He went about doing good and, in particular, curing all who were harassed and oppressed by [the power of] the devil, for God was with Him (Acts 10:38, *AMP.*).

The power and authority He possessed superseded all earthly power, rule and authority, and all the power of Satan. Through the divine power and authority He was given, He immediately began to exercise power and take dominion over Satan's power in the lives of those he had bound and oppressed. Jesus healed the sick, cast out devils and delivered all those who were oppressed by Satan's power.

WHAT IS IN HIS MOUTH?

One of the first accounts we have of Jesus after His forty days of prayer and fasting in the wilderness is in a synagogue casting a demon out of a man. The man cried out with a loud voice, "Let us alone; what have we to do with thee, thou Jesus of Nazareth? art thou come to destroy us? I know thee who thou art; the Holy One of God" (Luke 4:34).

Jesus was not intimidated by the presence of these evil spirits. He didn't hesitate. He spoke directly to the unclean spirit, rebuked him and commanded him to come out. "Hold thy peace, and come out of him" (Luke 4:35).

When the people saw Jesus cast out the demon, they were amazed and began talking among themselves. They said, "What a word is this! for with authority and power he commandeth the unclean spirits, and they come out" (Luke 4:36). In essence the people were saying, "What is in His words? What is in His mouth so that when He speaks demons bow, obey and come out? What is in His mouth?"

The word "authority" comes from the Greek word *exousia,* which means "the right to exercise." The words in Jesus' mouth were spoken with power and exousia, the right to exercise. The word "power" comes from the Greek word *dunamis,* which literally translated means "the miracle-working power of God." This is what the people said: "What is in His mouth? For with the right to exercise the miracle-working power of God, He casts out devils!" Evil spirits were subject to Jesus. They had to obey Him!

When Jesus rebuked this demon, He was taking authority over him and commanding him to go! He was forbidding the demon from controlling the man. He was demanding him to get his hands off and keep them off!

Think about it. Jesus was different from any man the people had ever seen. They had heard about and had been exposed to the prophets of God. But Jesus was different. When Jesus taught, He taught with authority. When He spoke, He spoke with power and authority. He spoke and the blind, the lame and the deaf were healed. He spoke and the evil spirits obeyed.

DIVINE POWER AND AUTHORITY!

Can you see yourself walking up to a blind person in your church or on the street and, without a long drawn-out prayer, speaking out the words, "In the name of Jesus, see"?

Can you see yourself walking down the street, stopping a person in a wheelchair and commanding him, "In the name of Jesus, get up out of that wheelchair and walk"?

Can you see yourself in a supermarket or shopping mall, when suddenly you hear an evil spirit call out your name and say, "I know who you are. You're one of God's anointed. Leave me alone. I know you are here to bind us and cast us out"? Then, can you see yourself speaking directly to the evil spirits, speaking the Word, rebuking them and commanding them to leave that person and not to come back? This is the power and authority Christ has given you! Jesus said,

> And these signs shall follow them that believe; In my name shall they cast out devils; they shall speak with new tongues; they shall take up serpents; and if they drink any deadly thing, it shall not hurt them; they shall lay hands on the sick, and they shall recover (Mark 16:17,18).

He said,

> He that believeth on me, the works that I do shall he do also; and greater works than these shall he do; because I go unto my Father. *And whatsoever ye shall ask in my name, that will I do, that the Father may be glorified in the Son* (John 14:12,13, emphasis added).

Jesus told His disciples,

> Behold! I have given you authority and power to trample upon serpents and scorpions, and [physical and mental

strength and ability] over all the power that the enemy [possesses]; and nothing shall in any way harm you (Luke 10:19, *AMP.*).

This is the God-given authority you have through the power of the Holy Spirit! You have the same power and authority Jesus demonstrated while He walked upon this earth 2,000 years ago! It's yours; it legally belongs to you. It's greater than any other power and authority known to man. It's a divine power and authority and Christ wants to activate it in your life and ministry through your prayers!

Not only do you have Christ's power and authority; He has also given you physical and mental strength! You don't have to be defeated in your thought life again. You don't have to be intimidated by the enemy telling you that your mind is so weak you can't overcome all the evil thoughts in this world.

 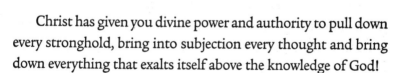

God has given you divine capability over all the enemy possesses!

Christ has given you divine power and authority to pull down every stronghold, bring into subjection every thought and bring down everything that exalts itself above the knowledge of God!

(For the weapons of our warfare are not carnal, but mighty through God to the pulling down of strong holds;) Casting down imaginations, and every high thing that exalteth itself against the knowledge of God, and bringing into captivity every thought to the obedience of Christ (2 Cor. 10:4,5).

He has given you divine capability over *all* the enemy possesses! *Nothing* shall in any way harm you!

All the power and authority Jesus has in His position is invested in His Church! "Far above all principality, and power, and might and dominion, and every name that is named, not only in this world, but also in that which is to come" (Eph. 1:21).

Satan is defeated!

Jesus faced and defeated him on the cross. "[God] disarmed the principalities and powers that were ranged against us and made a bold display and public example of them, in triumphing over them in Him and in it [the cross]" (Col. 2:15, *AMP.*).

SATAN FEARS THE CHURCH!

Satan knows that we have been given the power and legal right and authority not only to bind him and the evil principalities attacking our families and holding people in our cities and nations in bondage, but also to completely destroy his strongholds and loose all those who are bound by his power.

He fears the day the Church begins to rise up in the full power and authority of Jesus' name because he knows he will have to retreat!

The disciples and believers in the Early Church exercised the power and authority of Jesus' name. There was such a demonstration of God's miracle power that they laid the sick in the streets on beds and couches so that Peter's shadow would fall on them and they would be healed (see Acts 5:15).

The power wasn't in Peter or the other disciples. They weren't going in their own power and authority. They spoke healing and cast out demons in the power and authority of Jesus' name. In the power and authority in Jesus' name they took dominion and established the kingdom of God wherever they went.

This is what God intends the Church to do today. Under

this prayer anointing that is being released, He wants to raise us to a new dimension of power and authority through our prayers where we are enforcing Christ's victory and taking dominion.

We have a legislative branch in the United States government with legislators who establish law and order. All truth is parallel. We are the legislators of the kingdom of God! *We decree law and order!* We establish the will of God! We take dominion and declare "Thy Kingdom come, Thy will be done" (see Matt. 6:10) in our cities and nations. We are part of another dimension and we rule and reign through the power and authority of Jesus Christ!

As this prophetic prayer anointing is released, God will bring us into a new dimension of strategic warfare prayer where we are exercising the power and authority that legally belongs to us to demolish Satan's strongholds.

When Jesus prayed, all of heaven opened to Him and all of the resources of the kingdom of God were at His disposal. As we pray, all of heaven is at our disposal.

Jesus said, "The words that I speak unto you, they are spirit, and they are life" (John 6:63). His words, and not just the promises in His words, the *rhema* words He puts in your mouth are spirit and life!

Remember, your mouth is an instrument of authority to cause you to rule and reign in the presence of your enemies. Your words, anointed and imparted by the Holy Spirit as you pray, set dominion. The angels execute what you are saying. Through prayer we will change the spiritual atmosphere and the environment in our homes, in our churches and in our surroundings!

RECEIVE A NEW ANOINTING OF POWER AND AUTHORITY THROUGH PRAYER!

Beloved, I pray that even now, as you read this book, the Spirit of God will begin to open your eyes and reveal to you the position of power and authority Christ has given you through prayer.

I pray that He will release His power to flow through you as you pray in a greater dimension of that power and authority than you have ever experienced. I pray that the very words you pray will be quickened by the Holy Spirit, and that as you speak you will see a manifestation of God's power released to fulfill His promises and His will!

Now, let us join together in the Spirit to wage war with the principalities and powers that have been coming against you, your family and your finances. *Pray this prayer aloud in the power and authority God has given you through the Holy Spirit:*

In Jesus' name,

I break every bondage in and over my household. I tear down every enemy stronghold and bind every power and principality trying to bring my family into captivity. I pray seated with Christ in heavenly places and I rule and reign from that position of divine authority.

In Jesus' name, I come against every evil principality and spirit that has been trying to bind my finances and my ministry. I command you to loose your hold! "But my God shall supply all your need according to his riches in glory by Christ Jesus" (Phil. 4:19).

In Jesus' name, you must leave! The Word of God is against you. The blood of Jesus is against you! Spirits of drug abuse, alcoholism, adultery, profanity and immorality must go out of my house, out of my mind—I have the mind of Christ. I am free from the laws of sin and death. Sin does not rule or reign over me. I bind every spirit of strife and division and loose a spirit of love, joy and peace to fill my house.

My house belongs to God! The blood of Jesus is on my doorpost. I've been separated and redeemed, and I declare all my family shall be saved!

I lift up God's standard and shield over my house, over my family and over my ministry. I declare that nothing unholy or unlawful will enter to defile or harm me, my children, my grandchildren or any other member of my family.

In Jesus' name, we will walk in the strength and power of almighty God! We are set apart and dedicated to proclaim God's Word with power and authority, to pray for the sick and to set free those who are bound and oppressed by the devil, in Jesus' name!

CHAPTER

2

UNLIMITED SUPERNATURAL POWER SOURCE

The divine, energizing, supernatural power God intended to flow unhindered through the Church in this end-time hour is being released!

For thousands of years this power has remained a vast, untapped spiritual reservoir. While there have been a few choice servants of God who tapped into this supernatural power source through prayer, the vast majority of Christians still have not experienced its fullness in their lives.

One of the greatest examples of the power of prayer is revealed in the life of Elijah. This prophet was a mighty man of God whose prayers superseded the laws of nature. Through his prayers God revealed Himself as the all-powerful one and only true and living God! Elijah prayed and the heavens were shut so that it did not rain for three and one-half years. His prayer was not a long, drawn out prayer. It was a bold, daring prophetic declaration God directed him to make publicly before King Ahab.

King Ahab was one of the most evil rulers in Israel's history. He built a temple to Baal, set up an altar and appointed priests to lead people in worshiping Baal. "Ahab did more to provoke the Lord God of Israel to anger than all the kings of Israel that were before him" (1 Kings 16:33).

Elijah went to King Ahab and boldly declared, "As the Lord God of Israel liveth, before whom I stand, there shall not be dew nor rain these years, but according to my word" (1 Kings 17:1). In essence Elijah was saying, "The heavens are going to be shut up. There won't be any rain, not even dew upon the ground, except by the word God puts in my mouth!"

The words Elijah spoke were not his own, nor was he speaking in his own authority. His words were divinely anointed, directed and empowered by God! For three and one-half years there was no rain. There was a great famine throughout the land. During that time, Elijah was hidden away and supernaturally provided for by God. Then, at the appointed time, God spoke to Elijah, "Go, show thyself unto Ahab; and I will send rain upon the earth" (1 Kings 18:1). It was time for a divine confrontation!

Elijah went to King Ahab and directed him to call all the children of Israel and the 850 prophets of Baal together on Mount Carmel. There, God used Elijah's prayer to manifest His power and glory to Israel. He challenged the prophets of Baal and the children of Israel who had fallen into idolatry and were worshiping Baal. Elijah was neither fearful nor intimidated by King Ahab or the 850 prophets of Baal.

THERE WAS A SECRET POWER BEHIND ELIJAH'S PRAYERS

Elijah's faith and confidence were not in himself nor in any abilities he possessed. His unshakable faith and total dependence was on God Almighty! He had an intimate relationship with God and he knew God would do exactly as He had spoken. He knew God.

Elijah stood on Mount Carmel and challenged all of Israel, Queen Jezebel and all the 850 prophets of Baal. The sacrifice was prepared and the challenge given: "The God that answereth by fire, let him be God" (1 Kings 18:24). The prophets of Baal and all the people agreed together with him that the God who answered by fire was the one, true, living God.

From morning till noon, the prophets of Baal called on the name of Baal, but there was no answer. They leaped on the altar; they cut themselves with knives until the blood gushed out. There was no answer. They prophesied until evening. But there was still no answer; "There was neither voice, nor any to answer, nor any that regarded" (1 Kings 18:29).

Elijah repaired the altar of the Lord that was broken down, prepared the sacrifice and placed it on the altar. He commanded them to pour water over the sacrifice and the wood four different times until the sacrifice was soaked; the water ran off the altar and filled the trench around it. I believe the angels in heaven must have been watching, cheering Elijah on, ready to give a great shout of victory to the Lord!

What a scene! King Ahab and the 850 defeated, dejected prophets of Baal. One anointed prophet with the power and authority of God in his mouth.

ELIJAH'S PRAYERS SUPERSEDED NATURAL LIMITATIONS!

All eyes were on Elijah as he walked toward the altar. In my mind's eye I can see him as he lifts his hands, turns his eyes toward heaven and cries out to God with a mighty voice:

> Lord God of Abraham, Isaac, and of Israel, let it be known
> this day that thou art God in Israel, and that I am thy

servant, and that I have done all these things at thy word. Hear me, O Lord, hear me, that this people may know that thou art the Lord God, and that thou hast turned their heart back again (1 Kings 18:36,37).

Immediately, God answered by fire! The fire consumed not only the sacrifice, the wood, stones and the soil, but the water in the trenches as well. God's power and glory were manifested! When the people saw the fire, they fell prostrate on their faces and cried out, "The Lord—he is God! The Lord—he is God!" (1 Kings 18:39, *NIV*).

Some time later we see Elijah praying for the heavens to open and the rain to fall. He is kneeling on Mount Carmel with his face between his knees. In expectation of the fulfillment of God's promise to send rain, he sends his servant to look toward the sea for signs of rain.

Elijah's servant returns with the report: "There is nothing." Six times Elijah sends his servant out and six times he comes back with the same report: "There is nothing." On the seventh time the servant returned and told Elijah, "A cloud as small as a man's hand is rising from the sea."

So Elijah said, "Go and tell Ahab, 'Hitch up your chariot and go down before the rain stops you' " (1 Kings 18:44, *NIV*).

Regardless of the natural circumstances he faced, Elijah's faith never wavered. He didn't stop praying. He persevered in prayer. As he prayed, he *believed* and *expected* God's promise of rain to be fulfilled. Elijah's prayers were divinely energized! Elijah was a man with the same natural limitations that we have. He was subject to the same feelings we experience: discouragement, pain, sorrow and fear. Yet he prayed and the heavens were opened.

Elijah was a human being with a nature such as we have [with feelings, affections, and a constitution like ours]; and he prayed earnestly for it not to rain, and no rain fell on the earth for three years and six months. And [then] he prayed again and the heavens supplied rain and the land produced its crops [as usual] (Jas. 5:17,18, *AMP.*).

Notice the key to God's supernatural power that was released and caused the heavens to open and the rain to fall. James wrote, "The earnest (heartfelt, continued) prayer of a righteous man makes tremendous power available [dynamic in its working]" (Jas. 5:16, *AMP.*).

Elijah's prayers superseded natural limitations! As a result of his prayers, the heavens opened, and after three and one-half years the rain fell!

The same power in prayer is available to us today. The prayers of the righteous on behalf of their families, cities and nations makes tremendous power available—dynamic in its working!

A NEW LEVEL OF POWER AND AUTHORITY IN OUR PRAYERS!

God intends this same kind of power and authority in prayer that was manifested in Elijah's life to be experienced in the lives of His people today. He is going to raise up men and women like Elijah who pray with the power and authority of God to fulfill His will upon the earth!

Receive this prophetic word into your spirit!

God is releasing a powerful prayer anointing upon the Church. As God's people turn away from their own self-sufficiency, their reliance upon the arm of the flesh, and yield themselves totally to the Holy Spirit, they will pray bold, prophetic prayers.

As they pray, God's power and glory will be manifested in the nations as a witness to the world of God's unlimited power.

The prayers they pray will be divinely directed and empowered by the Holy Spirit to fulfill God's desires and purposes. They will supersede natural laws and limitations.

As God's people begin to flow under this prayer anointing and begin to pray prayers that are directed from the very heart of God, the fire of the Spirit will once again fall upon the Church.

This prophetic prayer anointing will not be released upon everyone. There will be Christians who will be unwilling or afraid to let go of their preconceived ideas and man-made traditions and doctrines to step into the new fresh flow of God's Spirit. They will cling to the past and rely upon their limited understanding instead of abandoning themselves in full surrender to the direction and anointing of the Holy Spirit.

Christians walking in close communion and fellowship with Christ, who are fully dedicated and consecrated to fulfilling His will, who are walking in obedience to His Word and who are willing to allow the Holy Spirit free reign in their lives will be able to receive this new prophetic prayer anointing.

Their spiritual senses will be increased. They will see and hear things in the Spirit they have never seen or heard. They will walk in a new realm of revelation, faith and boldness to pray prophetic prayers and to believe God for the impossible.

Are you ready to receive this end-time prophetic prayer anointing? Are you ready to move into a new dimension of prayer where you will see and hear things in the Spirit you have never seen or heard? Do you want to walk in a new realm of revelation, faith and boldness to pray prophetic prayers and believe God for the impossible? If you are ready and willing to dedicate yourself wholly to God and give the Holy Spirit free reign in your life, get ready to receive this new prophetic prayer anointing God is releasing now!

When we look at the tremendous power that was manifested through the prayers of Elijah and other anointed servants of God in the Old Testament and the Early Church, and compare it with the experience of the vast majority of Christians today, it is difficult to understand how we can have that same supernatural power released through our prayers.

Moses prayed and God manifested supernatural signs and wonders to deliver the children of Israel out of bondage. When God was ready to wipe out every trace of the children of Israel because of their rebellion and disobedience, Moses fasted and prayed for forty days and God changed His mind and Israel was spared (see Exod. 32:9-14).

Joshua prayed and the sun and moon stood still. Joshua spoke to the Lord in the presence of the children of Israel, " 'O sun, stand still at Gibeon, and O moon in the valley of Aijalon.' So the sun stood still, and the moon stopped, until the nation avenged themselves of their enemies" (Josh. 10:12,13, *NASB*).

Elijah and Elisha prayed and the dead were raised! (see 1 Kings 17:22; 2 Kings 4:35). Isaiah prayed and brought the shadow of the sun back 10 degrees! (see 2 Kings 20:11). King Hezekiah prayed for deliverance out of the hands of his enemy, King Sennacherib, who had come with his massive army to destroy the children of Israel. The angel of the Lord delivered them and killed 185,000 Assyrians in one night! (see 2 Kings 19:35).

THE GOD WHO ANSWERS BY FIRE!

Throughout the Old Testament, God proved Himself as the only true and living God who hears and answers the prayers of His people. The one major distinguishing factor between the children of Israel and the other nations and their idols was that they served the God who heard their prayers and who manifested His supernatural power on their behalf.

Why do you think the enemies of Israel trembled when Israel marched against them? Israel didn't have sophisticated weapons. They were never a majority, but when the heathen kings heard, "Here come the Jews," they trembled!

The heathen kings said, "We have gods, but they are deaf. We have gods but they are blind. We have gods but they go on journeys. We cut ourselves, we lay our children on the altars and burn them, but we get no answers to our prayers. But, here come the Jews, whose God hears and answers prayers. He parts water. He feeds in the wilderness. He quenches the violence of fire. Look out, here come the Jews!"

The testimonies of Abraham, Isaac, Jacob, Moses, Joshua, Elijah, Elisha, Samuel, David, Daniel, Isaiah and all the other Old Testament saints still speak today. They cannot be denied. Hear Moses' testimony: "Know therefore that the Lord thy God, he is God, the faithful God, which keepeth covenant and mercy with them that love him and keep his commandments to a thousand generations" (Deut. 7:9).

Hear David's testimony and confidence in the faithfulness of God to hear and answer Him: "I cried unto the Lord with my voice, and he heard me out of his holy hill. I laid me down and slept; I awaked; for the Lord sustained me" (Ps. 3:4,5).

Hear David's testimony again: "In my distress I called upon the Lord, and cried unto my God: he heard my voice out of his temple, and my cry came before him, even into his ears" (Ps. 18:6).

Listen to the testimony of King Solomon as he stood before the children of Israel: "Blessed be the Lord, that hath given rest unto his people Israel, according to all that he promised: there hath not failed one word of all his good promise, which he promised by the hand of Moses his servant" (1 Kings 8:56).

God promised to hear and answer His people. He spoke through the prophet Zechariah, "They shall call on my name, and I will hear them: I will say, It is my people: and they shall say, The Lord is my God" (Zech. 13:9).

God promised through Isaiah, "Before they call, I will answer; and while they are yet speaking, I will hear" (Isa. 65:24).

When Jeremiah was in prison God promised him, "Call unto me, and I will answer thee, and show thee great and mighty things, which thou knowest not" (Jer. 33:3).

From Genesis to Malachi we have an indisputable record of the mighty God who not only hears the prayers of His people, but who also supernaturally intervenes and manifests His power in response to their prayers. Throughout the ages, there is not one record of anyone who ever came to God in faith and in accordance with His will who went away without receiving the answer needed from Him.

FIX YOUR FAITH ON THE GOD WHO HEARS AND ANSWERS PRAYER!

The God you and I serve today is the Almighty God Jehovah who not only hears, but always *answers* prayer! This is the very foundation for all our prayers and intercession. When we look at the faithfulness of our God and know that with Him there is absolutely no margin for failure, we have no doubt that He will hear and answer our prayers.

Listen to David's testimony: "The eyes of the Lord are upon the righteous, and his ears are open unto their cry. The righteous cry, and the Lord heareth, and delivereth them out of their troubles" (Ps. 34:15,17).

Not only do we *know* that God hears our faintest cry, but we also know that He looks for the opportunity to manifest His power on our behalf! "For the eyes of the Lord run to and fro throughout the whole earth, to show himself strong in the behalf of them whose heart is perfect toward him" (2 Chron. 16:9).

Whenever we pray, our faith must be fixed upon our God, His almighty power and His faithfulness to us. Without this strong foundation of simple faith in God, that you know He will hear and answer your prayers, you might as well not even pray. "But without faith it is impossible to please him: for he that cometh to God must believe that he is, and that he is a rewarder of them that diligently seek him" (Heb. 11:6).

When you really know God intimately, your faith will never waver. Regardless of the circumstances you face or the size of the mountain of your need, you will be able to come to Him in prayer, *knowing* He will hear your cry and meet your need. Think about the power that was manifested in response to the prayers of Moses, Joshua, Elijah, Elisha and the other men and women of faith in the Old Testament. They were able to tap into the supernatural miracle-working power of God through their prayers because of their relationship with God. They were living in covenant relationship with Him based upon their covenant with Him and the promises He had given them.

Their prayers were accepted, not upon the basis of any personal merit of their own, but upon the basis of their loyalty and faith in God that He was the one true and living God and that He would do all that He had promised. As long as they loved, served and obeyed Him, they were able to claim all the promises of the covenant. However, when they continually turned their backs on Him and rebelled against Him, He refused to hear them. Sin separated them from Him.

David said, "If I regard iniquity in my heart, the Lord will not hear me: But verily God hath heard me; he hath attended to the voice of my prayer. Blessed be God, which hath not turned away my prayer, nor his mercy from me" (Ps. 66:18-20).

God's Word is clear. In Proverbs 15:29 we read, "The Lord is far from the wicked: *but he heareth the prayer of the righteous*" (emphasis added). Under the Old Covenant, the Old Testament people of God were able to approach God and be accepted by Him based upon their obedience. They did not have the blessed liberty and privilege we have today of entering into the very holy of holies through the blood of Jesus. They did not have the right as His children, redeemed by the precious blood of Jesus, to come boldly into His presence and cry out, "Abba, Father!" And they did not have the Holy Spirit, the third Person of the Trinity, living within them, giving them the power and authority to lay hold of the promises of God through divinely energized prayer!

UNLIMITED DIVINE ACCESS!

When most Christians think about the power of God that was manifested through Elijah (his calling forth fire from heaven, his shutting the heavens from pouring rain for three years, and the raising of the widow's son from the dead), it *is* possible for them to see God's power manifested through their prayers in the same powerful dimension.

Today, through the power of the Holy Spirit within us, we are able to confront the evil principalities and powers ruling over our cities and tear down their strongholds in the name of Jesus! "The weapons we fight with are not the weapons of the world. On the contrary, they have divine power to demolish strongholds" (2 Cor. 10:4, *NIV*). Through this new prayer anointing we will *demolish* strongholds of the enemy!

The apostle James wrote, "The earnest (heartfelt, continued) prayer of a righteous man makes tremendous power available [dynamic in its working]" (Jas. 5:16, *AMP.*).

Elijah was a mighty instrument in the hands of God, but, he was a man with feelings, affections and natural limitations just like us. He prayed earnestly according to what God had directed him to do and it released God's power.

> Elijah was a man just like us. He prayed earnestly that it would not rain, and it did not rain on the land for three and a half years. Again he prayed, and the heavens gave rain, and the earth produced its crops (Jas. 5:17,18, *NIV*).

If God manifested His mighty power in answer to Elijah's prayer and prophetic declaration, think about the awesome, unlimited power of God that will be released as God's people take their position of power and authority and begin to pray prayers that are divinely energized and directed by the Holy Spirit!

 Through this end-time prophetic prayer anointing, we will demolish strongholds of the enemy!

Have you ever considered the power of prayer in the lives of Moses, Elijah, Elisha, Joshua, Daniel or some of the other mighty men and women of faith in the Old Testament and thought,

- *If only I could pray like Elijah and see the dead raised.*
- *If only I could pray like Moses and see the awesome signs and wonders God manifested on behalf of Israel.*

- *If only I could talk with God face-to-face and have my face shine with the brightness of God's glory.*
- *If only I could pray like Daniel and receive the revelations he received concerning Israel and God's plan for the final climax of the ages.*

Under the Old Covenant, the Old Testament saints were limited in their prayers to the extent that they did not have the Holy Spirit living in them to divinely energize their prayers. They had only a limited measure, a small foretaste of what was yet to come through Christ. Neither were they able to approach the Father and pray in the power and authority of Jesus' name. As powerful as the prayers were of these Old Testament saints, think about the unlimited power of prayer that has been made available to you through Christ and the indwelling of the Holy Spirit.

Through Christ, you have been granted *unlimited divine access* to the very throne room of the Father! Through Christ, you have been elevated to a position of royalty in God's household as His child and joint heir with Christ! Through Christ, the Holy Spirit lives within you and you have the divine right and authority to pray in Jesus' name! Through the indwelling of the Holy Spirit there is available to you an *unlimited, supernatural power source* that is released through prayer.

GREATER WORKS THAN JESUS—UNLIMITED POWER!

Until Christ ascended into heaven and sent the Holy Spirit to live inside the disciples and believers, no one had ever been able to go before the Father in prayer and ask anything based upon the merit of Christ and the authority of His name. Jesus told His disciples, "Until now you have asked for nothing in My name; ask, and you will receive; that your joy may be made full" (John 16:24, *NASB*).

Knowing He was going back to the Father and that He was going to send the Holy Spirit to live inside them, giving them the power and authority in His name, Jesus told His disciples: "Verily, verily, I say unto you, He that believeth on me, the works that I do shall he do also; and greater works than these shall he do" (John 14:12).

Have you ever wondered how it would ever be possible for anyone to do greater works than Jesus did? Jesus made it very clear concerning who would do greater works than He had done. He did not limit these "greater works" to evangelists, prophets or ministers. He included all believers. All those who believe on Him will be able to do greater works. That includes you and me! But how is that possible?

Look closely at Jesus' words as He reveals *how* and *why*. Jesus said, "because I go unto my Father. And whatsoever ye shall ask in my name, that will I do, that the Father may be glorified in the Son" (John 14:12,13).

Beloved, Jesus has promised you *whatsoever* you ask in His name, He will do it! But Jesus didn't stop there. To remove any question the disciples may have had concerning this promise, Jesus said: "If ye shall ask any thing in my name, I will do it" (John 14:14).

He further qualified His promise to include *anything!* This word is all-inclusive. It doesn't need to be interpreted. It simply means *anything!* Whatever needs you may have in your life, whatever circumstances you are facing in which you need divine intervention from God, whatever crisis you may be facing in your family, in your finances or in your personal life, whatever spiritual desire you may have, whatever you want God to do for your city and nation is included under the word *anything* in this promise!

WHATSOEVER UNLIMITED!

Are you beginning to grasp the full significance of all that Christ was saying? The reason Jesus said that all those who believe on Him will do greater works than even He had done was because He was returning to the Father. In a few short hours He would go to the cross, face Satan and the powers of hell and defeat him. He was willingly laying down His life on the cross. Through His blood that would be poured out, man would be forever set free from the power of Satan.

The bondage of sin would be broken!

On the third day He would rise from the dead in great triumph. The works of the devil would be destroyed and He would be exalted to a position of supreme power and authority over all powers and principalities in heaven and in hell.

If you have any limitations in your mind concerning the unlimited power that God will manifest in response to your prayers, get rid of them!

When Christ returned to the Father, He would be given a name above every other name! "God exalted him to the highest place and gave him the name that is above every name, that at the name of Jesus every knee should bow, in heaven and on earth and under the earth, and every tongue confess that Jesus Christ is Lord, to the glory of God the Father" (Phil. 2:9-11, *NIV*).

Christ has entrusted within the lives of all true believers the same mighty power and authority that resides in His name. Through His name, demons must flee, sickness and disease must bow, the forces of nature must bow, everything must bow in submission to the power and authority of His name. Through the indwelling presence of the Holy Spirit and the power and authority of Jesus' name, you can do even greater works!

When you pray in the power and authority that is in Jesus' name, you are able to ask *anything* and He will do it!

PRAYING IN THE POWER AND AUTHORITY OF JESUS' NAME—UNLIMITED POWER!

If you have any limitations in your mind concerning the unlimited power that God will manifest in response to your prayers, get rid of them! This is a new day! God is releasing a new prayer anointing! We are moving into a higher dimension of prayer!

In addition to giving us the power and authority to pray in His mighty name, Jesus has anointed us with the Holy Spirit. After Jesus gave the promise that He will do whatsoever we ask in His name, He made another promise. He said, "If ye love me keep my commandments. And I will pray the Father, and he shall give you another Comforter, that he may abide with you for ever" (John 14:15,16).

Through the indwelling presence of the Holy Spirit, you are empowered to pray prayers that will break through every resistance of the enemy and release God's power to fulfill His will on earth!

In these final moments with His disciples, Christ emphasized over and over again the power and authority He has given us in prayer. This is the *unlimited* power that He has made possible for you through prayer! His promise to us today is:

Whatsoever we ask, in His name, He *will do it!*

Anything we ask, in His name, He *will do it!*

That same evening Jesus also told His disciples, "If you live in Me [abide vitally united to Me] and My words remain in you and continue to live in your hearts, *ask whatever you will, and it shall be done for you*" (John 15:7, AMP., emphasis added).

In this verse we see the key to tapping into the unlimited power of God to receive whatever we ask in prayer. That key is our relationship with Christ. The key is to know Christ intimately and to live in unbroken communion and fellowship with Him.

Jesus said, "Dwell in Me, and I will dwell in you. [Live in Me, and I will live in you.] Just as no branch can bear fruit of itself without abiding in (being vitally united to) the vine, neither can you bear fruit unless you abide in Me" (John 15:4, *AMP.*).

The type of intimate relationship Jesus was talking about is a moment-by-moment, day-to-day relationship. It is a relationship where we are no longer living our lives unto ourselves but are drawing our strength and sustenance from Him and His Word.

The apostle Paul summed up this intimate relationship when he said, "I am crucified with Christ: nevertheless I live; yet not I, but Christ liveth in me: and the life which I now live in the flesh I live by the faith of the Son of God, who loved me, and gave himself for me" (Gal. 2:20).

As long as you are abiding in Him, He said, *"Ask whatever you will, and it shall be done for you"* (John 15:7, *AMP.*, emphasis added).

Beloved, Christ has chosen and ordained you to walk in His power and authority where you are continually producing fruit. Jesus said, "Ye have not chosen me, but I have chosen you, and ordained you, that ye should go and bring forth fruit, and that your fruit should remain: that *whatsoever ye shall ask of the Father in my name, he may give it you*" (John 15:16, emphasis added). Again Christ promises *whatsoever you ask* the Father in His name He will give it to you!

A fifth time during His final moments with His disciples, Jesus leaves them with the promise that whatever they ask the Father in His name, the Father will give it to them. Jesus said: "And in that day ye shall ask me nothing. Verily, verily, I say unto you, *Whatsoever ye shall ask the Father in my name, he will give it you"* (John 16:23, emphasis added).

GOD IS MOVING US INTO A NEW DIMENSION OF STRATEGIC WARFARE PRAYER!

Beloved, it is time for the Church to take the mask off! Christ has given us an unlimited supernatural power source through prayer. He has given you the power and authority to pray in His name. He has invested in you all the power that is behind His name!

Christ sent the Holy Spirit to live inside of you, empowering you to do even greater works than He did! Through the anointing of the Holy Spirit, you have the same power to heal the sick, cast out devils, and raise the dead! The Church is God's delegated authority upon the earth. This delegated authority is absolutely inoperative outside the prayers of the Church. It works through the prayers of God's people.

We have limited the flow of God's power through us for too long! We have made excuses for too long! We have relied upon our own strength for too long! The vast majority of Christians have not yet come into this powerful dimension of prayer God intended for the Church. Get ready to receive an end-time prophetic prayer anointing!

God has planned to use the prayers of His Church to fulfill His purposes in the nations of the world before Christ returns. He intends to release His power through our prayers into our cities and nations to bring in the great end-time harvest of souls. He is going to use the anointed prayers of His people to wage war in the heavenlies to tear down and destroy the strongholds of the enemy that are holding entire cities and nations in bondage. However, before the Church can move into the position of power and authority God has planned and begin to operate in the unlimited power He has given us, something supernatural must happen!

God is now releasing a powerful end-time anointing upon the Church. This anointing will bring us into a new dimension of prayer where we will tap into His unlimited power to push back the forces of darkness—to press the battle in the power of His spirit until we see His kingdom come in every nation with every tribe, people and tongue having an end-time witness of the gospel.

Beloved, I pray for you right now that you will begin to sense God's Spirit stirring within you, preparing your heart to move into this new dimension of prayer. Pray this prayer aloud:

Father,

In the name of Jesus, I ask You to release a spirit of revelation upon me. Remove the spiritual cataracts from my eyes. Open my understanding to see the unlimited power You have ordained to flow through me in this end-time hour. Remove every natural limitation from my mind and every hindrance blocking the flow of Your Spirit in my life. Anoint my mind and spirit to hear and receive all that You are saying and directing me to do.

Release Your end-time prophetic prayer anointing upon me. Holy Spirit, I yield myself fully to You. Pray through me! Direct and empower my prayers. Anoint my mouth with fresh coals live from the altar so that I will pray and speak only the things You reveal and direct me to pray.

Use my prayers to pierce the darkness and destroy the strongholds of the enemy in my city and nation. Anoint me to pray prophetic prayers over my family, church, city and nation and enable me to take hold of Your prophetic promises for my life.

In the mighty name of Jesus!

CHAPTER 3

THE FUTURE BELONGS TO THE INTERCESSOR

The hour has come when God is positioning the Church, calling out intercessors and end-time spiritual warriors to wage war in the heavenlies on behalf of cities, people groups, nations and entire continents. One of the major distinctions of this end-time prophetic prayer anointing God is releasing is a new dimension of spiritual power and authority in our prayers.

God is going to bring us into a new dimension of authority in our prayers where our words, spoken with authority, invested in the promises of God, will enable us to confront every stronghold of the enemy! Not only is it important for you to *recognize* that God intends for you to operate in the same power and authority Christ demonstrated, it is also important for you to *pray* in a new dimension of power and authority.

Church, God is placing the future, the spiritual destiny of nations in our hands! The future will belong to those who walk in this new end-time prophetic prayer anointing to exercise power and dominion through prayer to take the nations for the kingdom of God!

There are many different types of prayer and they are all important! Under this new prophetic prayer anointing, there will be times when you will have a spirit of intercession and travail. You will weep for hours before the Lord. At times the intercession will be so strong you will feel like a woman in deep travail in the final agonizing moments before giving birth. At other times you will come into the presence of the Lord and just begin to pour out your heart in praise and worship. You will sing and dance before the Lord in your private time alone with Him. As you begin to worship, the bondages will break. A new strength and a new joy will begin to flow into your life. You will receive many answers to the prayers you have been praying for years as you pour out your heart to God in praise and worship for who He is and exalt His name.

Forget the religious, traditional approach to prayer. God wants to bring you into a completely new dimension of prayer where you totally abandon yourself and yield to His Spirit 100 percent. *Be willing to allow God to take you into new, uncharted spiritual territory!* If He directs you to weep and intercede for your city or places a burden on your heart for a particular group of people in some remote area of the world, be obedient and intercede. As you pray, expect God to speak to you and give you individual names of people, places and circumstances. He wants you to cover everything in prayer.

There will also be times when God will call on you to wage war in the heavenlies on behalf of cities and nations. As you pray in the Spirit, He will reveal specific names of demonic spirits and spiritual principalities that have established strongholds over cities, regions and groups of people. As you wage war in the Spirit, remember you are not facing these demonic forces in your own strength, but in the power and authority of the Holy Spirit within you. God is making you a warrior, and He has equipped you with everything you need to face the power of the enemy and tear down his strongholds.

God is saying to you, *The victory belongs to you, but you must declare it! You must pursue it with all diligence and perseverance! You must become violent!* "And from the days of John the Baptist until now the kingdom of heaven suffereth violence, and the violent take it by force" (Matt. 11:12).

He is giving you His promise and assuring you: *You are the victor! You are the aggressor! The power I am releasing within you assures you that you will not be defeated; you will overcome even as I have overcome!*

As you pray in the Spirit and begin to confront these principalities and tear down strongholds in Jesus' name, the Holy Spirit will anoint you to pray prophetic declarations over people, places and nations. You will know they are prophetic declarations because they will not be according to man's wisdom but will be directed by God to fulfill His purposes. "Likewise the Spirit also helpeth our infirmities: for we know not what we should pray for as we ought: but the Spirit itself maketh intercession for us with groanings which cannot be uttered" (Rom. 8:26).

As you pray these prophetic declarations, it will release a flow of God's power to bring them to pass. The future belongs to the intercessors!

GOD'S PROPHETIC PURPOSE
FOR PRAYER TODAY

To move into this new dimension of strategic warfare prayer and be used by God to impact cities and nations through deep intercession and strategic spiritual warfare, you need to have a revelation of the important role that the prayers of God's people have in relationship to prophetic end-time events.

In the book of Revelation God reveals to us how the prayers of His people are a major key in the unfolding of His end-time plan. In a vision, John is taken to the throne room of heaven where he sees a seven-sealed scroll. John said, "Then I saw in the right hand of him who sat on the throne a scroll with writing on both sides and sealed with seven seals" (Rev. 5:1, *NIV*).

This scroll reveals God's end-time plan and the events that will take place on the earth. A search is made throughout heaven for one who is worthy to break the seals and open the book. After searching through the heavens, the Mighty Conqueror, the Lion of the tribe of Judah, the root of David steps forward and takes the book. Since Christ conquered Satan and won the victory over sin, death and hell, He alone has the right to open the book and break the seals.

But look closely at Revelation 5:8: "And when he had taken the book, the four beasts and four and twenty elders fell down before the Lamb, having every one of them harps, and golden vials full of odours, which are the prayers of saints." It is very significant that *before* the seals are broken and the awesome end-time judgments of God begin, the prayers of God's people are offered up with incense mingled together with praise to God.

We see this again in Revelation chapter 8. *Before* the seven trumpet judgments of God are released upon the wicked, the prayers of God's people are first offered to God on the golden altar before His throne. John said,

> And I saw the seven angels which stood before God; and to them were given seven trumpets.
>
> And another angel came and stood at the altar, having a golden censer; and there was given unto him much incense, that he should offer it with the prayers of all saints upon the golden altar which was before the throne.
>
> And the smoke of the incense, which came with the

prayers of all the saints, ascended up before God out of the angel's hand. And the angel took the censer, and filled it with fire of the altar, and cast it into the earth: and there were voices, and thunderings, and lightnings, and an earthquake (vv. 2-5).

In both of these chapters involving the unfolding of God's plan, the prayers of God's people ascend to His throne before any judgment begins.

Beloved, our prayers here on earth on behalf of the lost, our cries to Him regarding the wickedness and immorality surrounding us, our prayers against the evil forces unleashed on the world today, and for God's intervention on our behalf, are not forgotten. They ascend before God, and are as a sweet-smelling incense in His nostrils.

God is anointing and placing intercessors in strategic positions around the world.

In response to the cries and prayers of the saints, the angel in Revelation chapter 8 takes the censer, fills it with fire, and casts it down to the earth (see v. 5). These prayers release the angels to sound the seven trumpets, which unleashes the judgments of God upon the wicked.

It isn't until the prayers of God's people are offered to Him that the angels are released to sound the trumpets and God's judgments come upon the world. The angels are God's means of administering the victory, but it will be the saints and the prayers of the saints who win the final victory.

Before Christ returns, God will to use the prayers of His people to break down Satan's strongholds and open nations that have been closed to the gospel for many years.

PRAYER THAT CHANGES THE SPIRITUAL DESTINY OF CITIES AND NATIONS

The future belongs to the intercessor!

God is anointing and placing intercessors in strategic positions around the world and is commissioning them to stand in the gap for cities and nations. He is calling them to wage war in the Spirit and to tear down the enemy's stronghold through strategic warfare prayer.

God is sounding an alarm. He is raising up men and women who will humble themselves before Him through fasting and prayer until they see entire cities and nations won for the kingdom of God.

You may wonder, *Is it really possible to take a city through prayer? Is it really possible that prayer and fasting can change the spiritual destiny of a city or a nation and that God will pour out His Spirit and multitudes be won into His kingdom?*

The great city of Nineveh, with 60,000 people, was spared because they heard the warning of Jonah, the prophet, and repented. God sent Jonah to warn the people of His coming judgment. Jonah cried out, "Yet forty days, and Nineveh shall be overthrown" (Jon. 3:4).

When the people and the king of Nineveh heard the warning from the prophet of God, they proclaimed a fast. The king took off his royal robes, clothed himself in sackcloth and sat in ashes as an outward sign of his repentance. He proclaimed a decree throughout the land, saying,

Let neither man nor beast, herd nor flock, taste any thing: let them, not feed, nor drink water: But let man and beast be covered with sackcloth, and cry mightily unto God: yea, let them turn every one from his evil way, and from the violence that is in their hands. Who can tell if God will turn and repent, and turn away from his fierce anger, that we perish not? (Jon. 3:7-9).

The entire city of Nineveh fasted and prayed and repented. It was a citywide revival! The people turned from their evil ways and turned back to God. God heard their prayers and saw their works, "and God repented of the evil, that he had said that he would do unto them; and he did it not" (Jon. 3:10).

Through Moses' intercession, the entire nation of Israel was saved from destruction. When the children of Israel turned their backs on God and sinned against Him by worshiping the golden calf they had made, God was ready to completely destroy them. He told Moses, "Let me alone, that I may destroy them, and blot out their name from under heaven: and I will make of thee a nation mightier and greater than they" (Deut. 9:14). Moses stood in the gap and cried out to God on behalf of the children of Israel:

"O Lord," he said, "why should your anger burn against your people, whom you brought out of Egypt with great power and a mighty hand? Why should the Egyptians say, 'It was with evil intent that he brought them out, to kill them in the mountains and to wipe them off the face of the earth'? Turn from your fierce anger; relent and do not bring disaster on your people. Remember your servants Abraham, Isaac and Israel, to whom you swore by your own self: 'I will make your descendants as numerous as the stars in the sky and I will give your descendants all this land I promised them, and it will be their inheritance forever' " (Exod. 32:11-13, *NIV*).

God listened to Moses' plea on behalf of the people and the Word says He "repented of the evil which he thought to do unto his people" (v. 14). Later, after Moses destroyed the golden calf and dealt with the people, he went up to Mount Horeb where he spent 40 days and nights fasting and praying on behalf of the people of Israel. During those 40 days he did not eat nor drink any water.

Here is a portrait of a true intercessor: Moses lying prostrate on his face before God pleading, "Oh, this people have sinned a great sin, and have made them gods of gold. Yet now, if thou wilt forgive their sin—; and if not, blot me, I pray thee, out of thy book which thou hast written" (Exod. 32:31,32). Moses stood in the gap between God and the children of Israel and asked Him to forgive their sins. He was willing to lay down his own life on their behalf.

Later at Kadesh-Barnea when the people rebelled against God and refused to go into Canaan and possess the land, Moses again interceded on their behalf. He again went up to Mount Horeb and spent forty days in fasting and prayer.

Can you see him there, lying prostrate on his face, before the Lord? His heart is broken because of the sins of the people. In his prayer he first pleads with God not to destroy His people whom He miraculously delivered out of Egypt. He cries out, "O Lord God, destroy not thy people and thine inheritance, which thou hast redeemed through thy greatness, which thou hast brought forth out of Egypt with a mighty hand" (Deut. 9:26).

Then, Moses reminds God of His covenant promise that He made to Abraham, Isaac and Jacob that He would multiply their seed and give them the land. He said, "Remember thy servants, Abraham, Isaac, and Jacob; look not unto the stubbornness of...their sin" (Deut. 9:27).

He called upon God to forgive the people according to His great mercy. "Pardon, I beseech thee, the iniquity of this people according unto the greatness of thy mercy, and as thou hast forgiven this people, from Egypt even until now" (Num. 14:19).

The Lord not only heard Moses' cries for the children of Israel, He answered, "I have pardoned according to thy word" (Num. 14:20). God acted in response to Moses' intercession. God's hand of mercy was extended and the nation of Israel was spared because of one man who was willing to be an instrument in the hands of God, to stand in the gap and intercede upon their behalf.

God would have wiped out every trace of the entire nation of Israel, "had not Moses his chosen stood before him in the breach, to turn away his wrath" (Ps. 106:23).

The future belongs to the intercessor!

PRAYERS CHANGE THE SPIRITUAL DESTINY OF *YOUR* CITY AND NATION

In this end-time hour God will use the prayers of His people to shake entire cities.

In response to our prayers, He will release a spirit of repentance and salvation. As the Church wages spiritual warfare against the ruling powers and principalities that are over its cities, spirits of lust, violence, hatred, immorality, drug and alcohol addiction, adultery, sexual perversion, worldliness and other demonic forces that have built strongholds and bondages will begin to break off people, and a spirit of conviction and repentance will be loosed!

God will use *your* prayers to impact cities and nations. Regardless of who you are, if you are willing to set yourself apart to fast and pray for your neighborhood, your city and nation, God will use your prayers to help bring revival and help bring in the end-time harvest of souls.

Charles Finney, who was used mightily by God to bring revival in the mid 1800s, told the following story about an old blacksmith whose prayers helped bring a powerful revival to his town.

In this town there had been no revival for many years. Spiritually, the town was dead. The people were unsaved.

There was an old blacksmith living in this town, who stammered so much it was painful to hear him speak. One day as he was working in his shop he became greatly burdened about the spiritual condition of the town and his church. The burden grew stronger and stronger until it seemed he could no longer bear it.

He locked the door to his shop and spent the afternoon in prayer, travailing before God on behalf of the spiritual condition of his town. He later went to his pastor and got his consent to conduct a meeting. The pastor agreed to let him hold a meeting but he didn't expect anyone to show up. When the time came for the meeting to start, the room filled to overflowing.

All was silent for some time. Suddenly, a sinner broke out in tears and begged someone to pray for him. Others followed. Later it was learned that people from every part of town were under deep conviction from the hour that the old blacksmith began praying in his shop.

God used an old stammering blacksmith who knew how to prevail in prayer to bring a powerful revival that shook the town and brought a harvest of souls into the kingdom of God.

Charles Finney was a mighty man of prayer. His ministry resulted in hundreds of thousands turning to the Lord. God used his meetings to help bring about one of the world's greatest revivals during the mid 1800s. As he traveled from city to city, two elderly men known as Father Clery and Father Nash accompanied him. When Finney went to Great Britain for several weeks of meetings, these two men went with him. They rented a dark, damp basement room for 25¢ a week and stayed there on their knees, prevailing in prayer. Their tears and travail were used by God to help bring revival and bring in a great harvest of souls in Great Britain and around the world.

The great revival that swept America in 1857-58 began when one man invited some people to pray with him at noon on September 23, 1857, in a Dutch Reformed Church in New York City. Gradually the crowds increased. The news concerning the prayer meeting spread to outlying cities and other prayer groups sprang up. After six months, 10,000 businessmen were meeting daily at noon in New York City alone. In eight months, from September until May, 50,000 people in New York City were saved and committed their lives to the Lord.

Prayer meetings began to spread across New England, down the Ohio Valley to Texas and across to the West Coast. A great portion of the United States and Canada was covered by a spirit of intercession. For two years there was an average weekly increase of 10,000 in membership in churches across America. And, it is estimated that out of a total U. S. population of 30 million at that time, one million came to Christ in this two-year period!

The future belongs to the intercessor!

BELOVED, GOD IS CALLING THE CHURCH BACK TO PRAYER!

Jesus said, "My house shall be called a house of prayer for all nations!" (Mark 11:17, *AMP.*). God is bringing us back to this purpose.

As this prophetic prayer anointing is being released, God is calling intercessors and churches to join together for corporate prayer meetings. He is directing pastors and Christian leaders to call for seasons of prayer and fasting.

These corporate prayer sessions, where Christians of all denominations unite together in prayer and spiritual warfare on behalf of their cities and nations, are a major key in destroying Satan's dominion over cities, releasing the miracle power of God and reaping a great end-time harvest of souls! Listen to this prophetic word:

> *This end-time prophetic prayer anointing will be so strong there will be prayer meetings that will continue for weeks and months at a time. There will be such a heavy burden and desire to see the lost won into the kingdom of God, people will spend all night in prayer. Many churches will remain open twenty-four hours a day with prayer going on continuously.*

In addition to these corporate prayer sessions, God is calling for a new dedication and commitment to individual intercession. He is calling intercessors to shut themselves away in "seasons" of prayer.

Corporate intercession is important, but unless we individually spend time daily in intimate prayer and communion with God, we will lack the power and authority to pray or lead corporate prayer. We will lack the power and authority to wage war in the heavenlies on behalf of our families, cities and nations.

The disciples in the Early Church lived continually under a heavy prayer anointing. As a result, the power and authority of God were released as they healed the sick, cast out devils and raised the dead.

When they faced a great need, it wasn't necessary for them to first go and get "prayed up" before they ministered to the need. When Peter was called to pray for Tabitha (in the Greek she is called Dorcas) who had already died, it was not necessary for him to get "prayed up."

Peter went immediately to her house where they had laid her dead body. After he put all the people out of the room, he kneeled down and prayed. Then, turning to the dead body he commanded, "Tabitha, arise" (Acts 9:40).

Think about the awesome power and authority Peter had through prayer. He spoke to a dead body and commanded life to enter back into it! It wasn't necessary for him to spend two or three hours in prayer to raise the dead. When he prayed, the Holy Spirit divinely energized the words coming out of his mouth because he lived continually under a heavy prayer anointing.

It is not God's will for us to raise every person who dies, but through this intimacy with God, Peter knew it was God's will for this to happen and he prayed in the will of God! Along with the other disciples, he had made a strong commitment to prayer.

Prayer was not *secondary* to the ministry God called him to do. To him it was inseparable from the work of the ministry. The disciples said, "But we will give ourselves *continually* to prayer, and to the ministry of the word" (Acts 6:4, emphasis added).

There were three time periods daily designated for prayer. The third hour of prayer was between the hours of 6:00 A.M. and 9:00 A.M.; the sixth hour was between the hours of 9:00 A.M. and 12:00 noon; the ninth hour was between the hours of 12:00 noon until 3:00 P.M. Peter and John were on their way to the Temple for prayer at the ninth hour when Peter saw the lame man lying at the gate of the Temple. He lifted him to his feet and said, "Silver and gold have I none; but such as I have give I thee: In the name of Jesus Christ of Nazareth rise up and walk" (Acts 3:6).

Peter and John lived in an atmosphere of prayer. They had already had two sessions of prayer that day. During these times designated for prayer, the disciples and believers prayed in their homes or in the Temple.

Cornelius was in his home praying about the ninth hour of the day, when an angel appeared to him in a vision and told him to send men to Joppa. The angel said, "Thy prayers and thine alms are come up for a memorial before God. And now send men to Joppa, and call for one Simon, whose surname is Peter: He lodgeth with one Simon a tanner, whose house is by the sea side: he shall tell thee what thou oughtest to do" (Acts 10:4-6).

At the sixth hour Peter went up on a housetop to pray (see Acts 10:9-15). While he was there he had a vision and God revealed to him not to call any man common or unclean. As he thought upon the meaning of the vision, God spoke to him and said, "Behold, three men seek thee. Arise therefore, and get thee down, and go with them, doubting nothing: for I have sent them" (Acts 10:19,20).

This is what I call divine communication! As Cornelius prayed, God gave him Peter's name, the location of his house and told him to send three men to bring him to Cornelius. Then, as Peter was in prayer on the rooftop, God revealed three men were coming and to go with them "doubting nothing." As a result of Cornelius's prayers, the Holy Spirit was poured out upon his household and all those he had gathered together. At midnight, Paul and Silas prayed, sang praises, and God supernaturally delivered them!

Paul prayed night and day for the believers in Thessalonica. He told them, "Night and day praying exceedingly that we might see your face, and might perfect that which is lacking in your faith" (1 Thess. 3:10). Once, on his way to the Temple to pray during the hour of prayer, a woman possessed with a spirit of divination came to Paul and he cast it out (see Acts 16:16-18).

Believers prayed in the Temple, in their homes, in prison, on riverbanks and wherever they went. "And on the sabbath we went out of the city by a river side, where prayer was wont to be made; and we sat down, and spake unto the women which resorted thither" (Acts 16:13).

God never intended prayer to be confined to the church building or places where Christians meet together. We need God to break through the religiosity that has attached itself to the Church! God intends us to live in an atmosphere of prayer whereby on any occasion, wherever we are, we pray as the Spirit directs us!

Whenever or wherever we see a need, we need to pray! Everywhere we go, we need to pray (not as a matter of form or to draw attention to ourselves) but because the Spirit within us yearns to pray through us. On the streets, at the supermarket, in our neighborhoods, on the job, in our schools—everywhere we go we should pray. Our prayers do not always manifest in an audible way. Our petitions can be prayed inside our spirits.

 Our prayers do not always manifest in an audible way. Our petitions can be prayed inside our spirits.

The Church was born in prayer. The supernatural power of God flowed through the disciples because they had a desire to pray and seek the face of God. They had the power to heal because they had the discipline to pray! They worked miracles because they worked on their relationship with God. They had victory in their hearts because they had hearts after God! They lived under a heavy prayer anointing because they had an intimate relationship with God.

GOD IS CALLING THE CHURCH TO REPENTANCE
FOR OUR LACK OF PRAYER

In the 52 years of ministry God has given me in the nations of the world, I have seen thousands accept Christ in a single service; I have seen blind eyes opened; I have seen deformed limbs straightened; I have seen cripples restored and all forms of diseases healed! I know beyond any doubt that the tremendous manifestation of God's power is the result of prayer.

Early in my ministry God gave me a revelation of the power of prayer, and I made a strong commitment to maintain my personal time alone with God, regardless of the cost. Every decision, every outreach, every action I feel God directing me to make is bathed in prayer. Day in and day out, long into the night and early in the morning, I get on my knees and cry out to a merciful God to save the lost, heal the sick and deliver the oppressed.

Many people do not understand me or the intensity of God's calling upon my life. Whenever I go to a city or nation to conduct meetings, I do not spend a lot of time with local pastors or scheduling other activities during the meeting. I have often been criticized for this.

Most of the time I shut myself in my room and spend hours in prayer seeking God, battling the spiritual forces of darkness and taking hold of victories God has for His people in prayer. God taught me that the battle is won in prayer before I ever step one foot into the stadium, arena or auditorium where the meeting is being conducted.

During the course of my ministry I spend hours alone daily with God. Many people wonder how it is possible that I keep the pace that I do year after year, without stopping. It's because I have learned to wait before God in prayer and intimate fellowship. That is when He strengthens and refreshes me. That is when He speaks to me and I receive the powerful revelations He gives me.

That is when God speaks to me about prophetic things that are coming in the world. That is when God paves the way for mighty revivals, signs, wonders and miracles to take place.

Many Christians never spend much time alone with God. They have never had a revelation while on their faces before God, shut in with Him, with His power being released into their lives. We cannot expect to win the world only through corporate prayer. We must have regular and special seasons of corporate prayer and fasting. But God is calling His people to a higher place of individual prayer. He is calling us to a place where our hearts beat with desire for fellowship and communion with Him.

This end-time call to prayer is not just for pastors, evangelists, ministers or Christian leaders. It is not just to those who are called to the ministry of intercession. God is calling every member of the Body of Christ to a higher level of commitment to:

1. Intimate communion and fellowship with Him in prayer.
2. Intercession and strategic warfare prayer for their cities and nations.

I call upon pastors, evangelists, ministers and church leaders to join me in leading the Church in repentance for our lack of prayer. God expects us to raise the standard and set the example in prayer. It's time to take the mask off!

Many pastors, ministers and Christian leaders have become so involved in ministry activities, conducting meetings, preaching, teaching, counseling, writing and running their churches and ministries, that they spend very little time in prayer. Prayer has become secondary in their ministry rather than being the heart and passion of their ministry.

As a result of this lack of prayer, they are operating in their own strength. The anointing and power of God is not flowing through them in the dimension it must for true successful ministry. Many have come to a place of "spiritual burnout." Jesus taught a parable, "that men ought always to pray, and not to faint" (Luke 18:1). Most often the reason for spiritual burnout is a lack of prayer. Jesus essentially said, if you pray you won't faint!

I must warn you. This is dangerous spiritual territory. There are many men of great faith who have fallen during a time of great ministry activity because of their lack of commitment to prayer. This lack of prayerfulness is reflected in the experience of the great majority of Christians sitting in our church pews.

The average Christian spends more time watching television and being involved in personal pursuits than he does in prayer. There are Christians who have so neglected their prayer life that they no longer have a will or desire to pray; there is no real joy in spending time alone with God. Others only pray as a last resort. They wait until they are in trouble to cry out to God.

God is calling the Church to a higher dimension in prayer where we are living under a new, heavy, end-time, prophetic prayer anointing. Forget the traditional concept of prayer! God desires to bring us into an experience in prayer where we are living in continual communion and fellowship with Him.

At His prompting, He wants us to be ready at any time to set aside time to spend in prayer and fasting on behalf of the lost in our communities, and tearing down strongholds in our cities and nations. As He reveals His will, He wants us to pray prophetic prayers over our personal lives, over our cities, over our governments and our nations that He will bring to pass in fulfillment of His plan and purposes.

In this end-time hour, God is looking for men and women, like the disciples in the Early Church, who will give themselves continually to prayer. He is calling us to accept our responsibility in prayer for our homes, our cities, our nations and the world.

Beloved, have you accepted the prayer responsibility for your home, city and nation?

GOD HAS APPOINTED YOU AS A SPIRITUAL WATCHMAN

As we look to Christ's coming, there is a very sobering question you and I must answer. When we stand before God, will there be blood on our hands?

We have an awesome responsibility before God. Knowing Christ is coming soon and that God's judgments are coming upon the world and all those who reject Christ, we have a solemn responsibility before God. We must not fail to warn and to intercede on behalf of the lost in our neighborhoods, cities, states and nations. God set Ezekiel as a spiritual watchman over the house of Israel and warned him:

> When I say to the wicked, O wicked man, you shall surely die, and you do not speak to warn the wicked from his way, that wicked man shall die in his perversity and iniquity, but his blood will I require at your hand. But if you warn the wicked to turn from his evil way and he does not turn from his evil way, he shall die in his iniquity, but you will have saved your life (Ezek. 33:8,9, *AMP.*).

The future belongs to the intercessor!

It is not just the responsibility of the preachers standing behind the pulpit to preach the Gospel and warn the wicked. God has called and commissioned every member of the Body of Christ to take their position as a spiritual watchman.

You are a spiritual watchman. Every day, there are people with whom you come in contact—on the job, at home, at school, in the supermarket and on the street—who are lost. Unless they are warned, repent, turn away from their sins, and turn to God, God's wrath will one day be poured out upon them.

Our minds cannot begin to comprehend the terrifying fear, the agony, the pain, the destruction that is coming upon the wicked as Christ returns to earth with the armies of heaven to tread the winepress of the fury of the wrath of God. "And out of his mouth goeth a sharp sword, that with it he should smite the nations: and he shall rule them with a rod of iron: and he treadeth the winepress of the fierceness and wrath of the Almighty God" (Rev. 19:15).

 Make no mistake about it—
judgment is coming!

It is hard to imagine the great slaughter that will take place during the battle of Armageddon, where the blood will flow as high as a horse's bridle for a distance of approximately 200 miles. "And the winepress was trodden without the city, and blood came out of the winepress, even unto the horse bridles, by the space of a thousand and six hundred furlongs" (Rev. 14:20).

Even in our wildest imaginations, we cannot picture the horrifying scene that will take place upon the earth as the seven vials of God's wrath are poured out.

THE CHURCH MUST SOUND THE ALARM IN PRAYER!

Make no mistake about it—judgment is coming! Untold millions will face these awful judgments and eternity in hell, unless you and I warn them. If ever there was a message that should motivate God's people to prayer—this is it!

God does not want us to sit back with our hands folded. He does not want us to become so caught up with the cares and worries of this life that we fail to see the signs of Christ's coming and we fail to intercede and warn those around us before it is too late.

As we see the Day of the Lord drawing near, we must sound the alarm and begin to intercede for the lost in our cities. We must cry out to God for mercy on their behalf, warn all those we possibly can of these coming judgments and give them the message of salvation, healing and deliverance in Jesus' name.

Think about your unsaved family members and friends, your neighbors and the multitudes of unsaved in your city. There are 6 billion people in the world today, but only 1 billion claim to know Jesus Christ as Lord and Savior. Billions of souls will slip into an eternity without the knowledge of Christ.

What have you done to warn them? Have you set aside time to fast and pray on their behalf? Will there be blood on your hands?

GOD IS CALLING THE CHURCH TO CONFESSION AND REPENTANCE

Today, the Church has entered into a new dimension of praise and worship and there is rejoicing, singing and dancing. We are seeing a greater freedom of the moving of the gifts of the Spirit. This is good and necessary. There is nothing I enjoy more than joining together with my brothers and sisters in worship in the presence of God.

However, it is *prayer* and *repentance* among God's people that is the real key to the releasing the great outpouring of His Spirit in these last days!

As the Body of Christ *unites* together in prayer,

• The Lord will "be jealous for his land, and pity his people" (Joel 2:18).

- Then He will hear from heaven and will forgive and heal our land (see 2 Chron. 7:14).
- Then will come times of rejoicing! (see Joel 2:23)
- Then will come restoration! (see Joel 2:25)
- Then will come blessing! (see Joel 2:26)

Multiplied millions of souls are at stake! And they will respond to our intercessions and our deep travail to release them from the clutches of Satan's hold.

God is raising up intercessors like Nehemiah and Daniel who mourned for the sins of Israel, fasted, prayed, confessed and repented. I want you to look for a moment at the prayers of these two great intercessors because I am convinced that God is calling the Church to not only stand in the gap, confess and lead our nations to repentance, but to also confess and repent for the sins we have committed and allowed to remain in the Church.

Nehemiah was the cupbearer of the Persian monarch, Artaxerxes. When he heard the report concerning the desolation of the city of Jerusalem, his heart was overcome with sorrow and he began to weep. Knowing that this desolation was brought upon the children of Israel because of their sins, he fasted and prayed, confessed and repented of their sins before God. Nehemiah prayed:

O Lord, God of heaven, the great and awesome God, who keeps his covenant of love with those who love him and obey his commands, let your ear be attentive and your eyes open to hear the prayer your servant is praying before you day and night for your servants, the people of Israel. I confess the sins we Israelites, including myself and my father's house, have committed against you (Neh. 1:5-7, *NIV*).

Nehemiah was a man of prayer with great spiritual vision. Not only did he see the natural destruction and condition of the people of Israel, but by faith he saw God's forgiveness and restoration. He proclaimed a fast and prayed day and night. He wept and grieved with godly sorrow over the sins of the people and their condition.

God wants you, as a man or woman of prayer, to have a new spiritual vision and burden for your family, church, city and nation. Not only does He want you to see the desperate conditions in your city and nation which have come as a result of sin, idolatry and rebellion against God, He wants you to see through the eyes of faith His forgiveness, healing, deliverance and restoration being poured out.

As you fast and pray, weep with godly sorrow over the sins of the people and their sinful condition. Then, through your prayers, stand before God on behalf of the people and confess their sins. "Godly sorrow brings repentance that leads to salvation and leaves no regret" (2 Cor. 7:10, *NIV*).

After you have confessed their sins, cry out to God for His mercy and forgiveness. Ask God to release a spirit of conviction for sin and to remove the spiritual blindness from people's eyes. As you pray, loose spirits of salvation and repentance and ask God to pour out a spiritual hunger upon the people.

After Nehemiah confessed the sins of the people of Israel, he reminded God of His covenant promise He made to Moses and the children of Israel. God warned them that if they were unfaithful, He would scatter them to the ends of the earth, but if they returned to Him and obeyed Him, He would forgive them and bring them back to their land.

Remember, I beseech thee, the word that thou commandedst thy servant Moses, saying, If ye trangress, I will scatter you abroad among the nations: But if ye turn unto me, and keep my commandments, and do them; though there were of you cast out unto the uttermost part of the heaven, yet will I gather them from thence, and will bring them unto the place that I have chosen to set my name there (Neh. 1:8,9).

Not only did Nehemiah pray, he put his prayers into action. He built the walls of Jerusalem *as he prayed.* Through prayer he overcame every obstacle. "Nevertheless we made our prayer unto our God, and set a watch against them day and night, because of them" (Neh. 4:9).

God heard Nehemiah's prayer and used Nehemiah to build up the walls around Jerusalem that were broken down, and to lead Israel to repentance and restoration.

The future belongs to the intercessor!

Daniel was a seasoned prayer warrior. He was a Jewish captive during the Babylonian captivity. When he understood from studying the Scriptures that the desolation of Jerusalem would last seventy years, he set himself to seek God's face through fasting and prayer.

Daniel said, "And I set my face to the Lord God to seek Him by prayer and supplications, with fasting and sackcloth and ashes; And I prayed to the Lord my God and made confession" (Dan. 9:3,4, *AMP.*).

After Daniel confessed the sins of the people, He cried out to God for mercy according to His righteousness. Listen to Daniel's prayer:

O my God, incline thine ear, and hear; open thine eyes, and behold our desolations, and the city which is called by thy name: for we do not present our supplications before

thee for our righteousness, but for thy great mercies.
O Lord, hear; O Lord, forgive; O Lord, hearken and do;
defer not, for thine own sake, O my God: for thy city and
thy people are called by thy name (Dan. 9:18,19).

Daniel pleaded for God's forgiveness for Israel based upon
God's righteousness and mercy, not upon any merit of his own
or that of the people.

Daniel's prayer was based on his deep-rooted faith and confidence in God. He knew God's faithfulness to keep His covenant
with His people. He said, "O Lord, the great and awesome God,
who keeps His covenant and lovingkindness for those who love
Him and keep His commandments" (Dan. 9:4, *NASB*). Daniel
knew the depth of God's forgiveness. He prayed, "The Lord our
God is merciful and forgiving, even though we have rebelled
against him" (Dan. 9:9, *NIV*).

Although they had sinned, Daniel knew God was a holy and
righteous God and he asked Him to turn away His anger from
Jerusalem. He said, "O Lord, in keeping with all your righteous
acts, turn away your anger and your wrath from Jerusalem, your
city, your holy hill" (Dan. 9:16, *NIV*).

As soon as Daniel began to pray, God heard him and dis-
patched an angel to give him understanding and *spiritual vision*
regarding what was going to happen to Israel and the things
which would take place during the end time.

SET YOUR SPIRITUAL FOCUS ON YOUR CITY AND NATION!

When Nehemiah and Daniel saw the desolate condition of
Israel, they immediately responded and moved into action.
Daniel "set his face" to seek the Lord through prayer and fasting

while Nehemiah began a fast and prayed to God day and night for the people of Israel.

Their spiritual vision was focused on seeking God through fasting and prayer, confession and repentance. They called on God's mercy for forgiveness. Even today, God is calling His people to take dominion through prayer as Daniel and Nehemiah did in the Spirit.

Are you taking your position of power and authority through prayer? Are you taking dominion over the evil principalities and powers of darkness trying to gain a stronghold in your family? Are you taking dominion over existing strongholds in your neighborhood, city and nation?

How long has it been since you looked at the condition of the lost in your city? How long has it been since you looked at the violence, crime, rape, murder, drug and alcohol addiction, pornography, and other bondages of Satan and wept with godly sorrow over the sins and wickedness of the people? How long has it been since your heart has been so burdened for your unsaved loved ones, coworkers and the lost within your city that you have consecrated yourself to God in fasting and prayer until you saw God's hand move on their behalf? What is your spiritual vision and burden for your family, your city and your nation?

The future belongs to the intercessor!

I pray for you right now that God will release upon you a new spiritual vision and burden for the lost within your city and nation. I pray that He will anoint your eyes so that you will be able to see your city and nation as He sees it and that your heart will be flooded by His great love and compassion toward those who are bound by Satan's power.

I pray that the Holy Spirit will direct and empower your prayers.

I ask the Father, in the name of Jesus, to release the power and anointing of the Holy Spirit upon you, enabling you to take dominion over the powers of darkness that have built strongholds in your city and nation. As you wage spiritual warfare against these evil principalities, I am believing God to destroy every stronghold and loose spirits of salvation, healing and deliverance in Jesus' name!

I pray that you will go forward in God's Spirit and His strength to reap a great harvest of souls!

POWER INTIMACY

A mighty, sovereign end-time call from God is being heard around the world! It is strong and unmistakably clear! Christ is calling His Church. He is calling you and me to a deeper level of intimacy with Him, a deeper level of prayer and intercession greater than anything we have ever experienced.

Do you hear it?

There is an insatiable desire and longing within my heart to know Christ in His fullness, to live in His presence, to behold His face, to walk with Him in close communion and fellowship. Is this the cry of your heart?

I am now entering my fifty-second year of ministry. From the depths of my innermost being there is a cry welling up within me: *Oh Lord, my heart longs for You. I long to see Your face and to behold You in all Your glory as I have never experienced before.*

I don't know about you, but there is nothing in this world that I desire. There is nothing holding me here. I want to see Jesus! Are you longing for the day when the heavens will unroll like a scroll and Christ will appear to carry His Bride away?

This intense longing and desire within us is the work of the Holy Spirit preparing the Bride for Christ's coming!

As this end-time prophetic prayer anointing is released, Christ will bring those who are ready to move into this new dimension of prayer first of all into a deeper intimacy with Him through prayer. We are witnessing the greatest prayer movement in the history of the Church! An estimated one hundred and eighty million Christians worldwide have made a commitment to pray for global revival and the fulfillment of the Great Commission.

This call to prayer is a call to the Church in preparation for Christ's coming. Only as we come into a place of intimacy with Christ, through prayer, will we truly know His heart and be empowered to complete the work He has called us to do. Remember this prophecy:

> *God is going to bring us into a new dimension of authority in our prayers where our words, spoken with authority, invested in the promises of God, will enable us to confront every stronghold of the enemy!*

Remember the prayer and heart cry of Paul: "That I may know him, and the power of his resurrection, and the fellowship of his sufferings, being made conformable unto his death" (Phil. 3:10).

God wants to release through our prayers power and authority that will impact cities and nations; He wants to give us power and authority that will demolish the last remaining strongholds of the enemy and help bring in the greatest harvest of souls in Church history. This power and authority will only be released as we enter into a deeper intimate relationship with Christ where we are living in unbroken communion and fellowship with Him.

In the prophecy God gave me at the beginning of the decade

of the '90s, He showed me that we would see and experience a great end-time outpouring of His Spirit. We are now seeing the beginning of this great end-time outpouring.

However, God also revealed that simultaneously His people will face the greatest confrontation and assault from Satan and his demon principalities that man has ever known or experienced. Why? Because even though Satan doesn't know the exact time, he knows his time is short.

As the Spirit of God poured this prophecy through me in 1990, I warned believers that as God's Spirit is working mightily through His people, Satan and his principalities will be working to hinder and stop the work of God. Christians who do not recognize what is happening or do not know how to exercise spiritual authority over Satan will be overwhelmed. They will be unable to stand. They will be taken by surprise.

POWER DOESN'T TRAVEL IN WORDS, BUT IN RELATIONSHIPS!

There are many Christians who are right now involved in the greatest satanic assault they have ever experienced. They are being attacked in every possible area of their lives. At times, it seems that all hell has been loosed against their physical bodies, against their families, against their finances and against their ministries.

As this end-time prophetic prayer anointing is released, God will show you the attacks of the enemy before they occur, and you will engage spiritual forces by *offensive* warfare prayer. Your victory in overcoming these satanic assaults is dependent on one thing—your relationship with Christ.

A powerful truth God has been using me to teach is *power intimacy!* Power does not travel through words. Power travels in relationships. By His Spirit God is calling the Church into this new dimension of power intimacy with Him. Through prayer God will prepare us to face every circumstance and every satanic assault with the assurance of 100 percent victory!

Through prayer God will prepare us to face every circumstance and every satanic assault with the assurance of 100 percent victory!

Hear me carefully. Only those who come into this deeper level of intimacy with Christ, where they are vitally united together with Him through a day-by-day, moment-by-moment relationship, where they are waiting before Him in prayer, will be able to stand.

The power and authority in prayer that flowed through Moses was the result of his relationship with God. This relationship brought a manifestation of God's supernatural power in parting the Red Sea, raining manna from heaven, causing water to gush forth from a rock, and delivering the children of Israel out of the hands of their enemies.

The power and authority in prayer that flowed through Elijah to call down fire from heaven, raise the dead and part the Jordan River, demonstrating to the world that the God of Abraham, Isaac and Jacob was the one true and living God, was the result of his relationship with God Almighty!

The power and authority in prayer that was manifested in the lives of Peter, Paul and the other disciples in the Early Church that enabled them to heal the sick, cast out devils and raise the dead, demonstrating to the world that Jesus is Who He claims to be, the Son of the living God, was the result of their relationship with Christ.

Power doesn't travel in words. Power travels in relationships! It was not simply the words Moses spoke. God did not answer his prayers because of what he said. Moses did not follow a "formula" for his prayers. He did not depend on his natural abilities or powers of persuasion to change God's mind.

Beloved, forget methodology. Methodology will not get the job done! Forget strategies. Strategies will not suffice!

Moses had a deep, intimate relationship with God. He was known as the friend of God. Moses found favor in God's sight. The Lord knew him face-to-face. "And the Lord spake unto Moses *face to face*, as a man speaketh unto his friend. I know thee by name, and thou hast also found grace in my sight" (Exod. 33:11,12, emphasis added).

Moses *knew* God. He knew the depth of God's love and mercy and prayed according to the divine character of God. He told God, "The Lord is long-suffering and slow to anger, and abundant in mercy and loving-kindness....Pardon, I pray You, the iniquity of this people according to the greatness of Your mercy and loving-kindness, just as You have forgiven [them] from Egypt until now" (Num. 14:18,19, *AMP.*).

Later, when God commanded Moses to go in and take possession of the land, He told Moses that His presence would not go with the children of Israel. Moses went to the Tabernacle where God's *Shekinah* glory came down and there he talked with the Lord "face to face." He told God:

Thou hast said, I know thee by name, and thou hast also found grace in my sight. Now therefore, I pray thee, if I have found grace in thy sight, show me now thy way, that

I may know thee, that I may find grace in thy sight: and consider that this nation is thy people (Exod. 33:12,13).

God answered Moses' prayer because of His covenant relationship with him. He told Moses, "I will do this thing also that you have asked, for you have found favor, loving-kindness, and mercy in My sight and I know you personally and by name" (Exod. 33:17, *AMP.*). Moses' hunger for God resulted in God revealing more of Himself to him.

WE HAVE DIVINE ACCESS TO THE HOLY OF HOLIES!

The basis and foundation for all your prayer and intercession is your personal intimate relationship with the Lord. As a child of God, born of His Spirit, He knows you intimately by name. You have received the Spirit of adoption, where you can cry "Abba, Father" (Rom. 8:15).

You have *unlimited divine access* to the very throne room of God! Whatever needs you may have, you can go boldly into His presence and cry out, "Abba, Father," and know He will hear you. One of the greatest keys in unlocking the power of prayer is knowing the strong position you have in gaining divine access, entering the holy of holies, and appropriating God's promises for your life.

When we enter into God's presence and commune with Him, He does not want us to come *hoping* or *presuming* He will hear and answer our prayers. He expects us to come *boldly*, without fear or doubt, knowing that, through Christ, we have been granted legal access to His throne room; and He will not only hear us, but He will also give us those things we need and have desired of Him.

Inasmuch then as we have a great High Priest Who has [already] ascended and passed through the heavens, Jesus the Son of God, let us hold fast our confession [of faith in Him]. For we do not have a High Priest Who is unable to understand and sympathize and have a shared feeling with our weaknesses and infirmities and liability to the assaults of temptation, but One Who has been tempted in every respect as we are, yet without sinning. Let us then fearlessly and confidently and boldly draw near to the throne of grace (the throne of God's unmerited favor to us sinners), that we may receive mercy [for our failures] and find grace to help in good time for every need [appropriate help and well-timed help, coming just when we need it] (Heb. 4:14-16, *AMP.*).

Through His Spirit living within you, you are no longer an outcast, but a member of the family of God. The Spirit within you bears witness with your spirit that you are a child of God. And as a child of the Most High God, you can not only approach Him, but you can also cry, "Abba, Father."

For ye have not received the spirit of bondage again to fear; but ye have received the Spirit of adoption, whereby we cry, Abba, Father. The Spirit itself beareth witness with our spirit, that we are children of God: And if children, then heirs; heirs of God, and joint-heirs with Christ (Rom. 8:15-17).

When you pray, you cannot come to God based on your own merit, your righteousness, your good works, or your sacrifices. The only way you can approach God and know, beyond any doubt, that He has heard you and will do what you have asked is through your relationship with Christ.

Paul wrote to the Hebrews, "But without faith it is impossible to please him: for he that cometh to God must believe that he is, and that he is a rewarder of them that diligently seek him" (Heb. 11:6).

The apostle James added, "But let him ask in faith, nothing wavering. For he that wavereth is like a wave of the sea driven with the wind and tossed. For let not that man think that he shall receive any thing of the Lord" (Jas. 1:6,7). The only way you are able to receive answers to your prayers is to have a strong, unwavering faith that is based on knowing God and knowing what Christ your great High Priest has provided for you.

When you come before God in prayer, He does not want you to be fearful, wishy-washy or wondering if He will answer your prayers. He expects you to come to Him with holy boldness and complete confidence, knowing that through Christ you have direct access into the holy of holies where you can draw near to Him, where you can know Him intimately, where you can receive from Him all that you need.

Praise God! We have a great High Priest, sitting on the right hand of the Father, who ever lives to make intercession for us! He is there now making intercession for you and me! "But this man, because he continueth ever, hath an unchangeable priesthood. Wherefore he is able also to save them to the uttermost that come unto God by him, seeing he ever liveth to make intercession for them" (Heb. 7:24,25).

Because of Christ's blood, which He shed on Calvary for the atonement of our sins, we have the privilege and right to boldly enter into the most holy place, the very holy of holies, where God in all His power and glory dwells.

Based on Christ's blood, we have the boldness and assurance that God will answer our prayers. There can be no greater assurance! His blood is all-sufficient for all our needs for all time! The apostle Paul wrote to the Hebrews, "Having, therefore, brethren, boldness to enter into the holiest by the blood of Jesus, by a new and living way, which he hath consecrated for us, through the veil, that is to say, his flesh" (Heb. 10:19,20). Knowing that we have this great High Priest,

- Who became like us, taking upon Himself the form of flesh and blood;
- Who knows our pain and weaknesses;
- Who shed His blood so we could be reconciled to the Father;
- Who feels for us in our infirmities; we can come before God with a bold, daring and unwavering faith.

The apostle Paul said, "Let us therefore come boldly unto the throne of grace, that we may obtain mercy, and find grace to help in time of need" (Heb. 4:16).

NO MORE WAVERING, QUESTIONING OR STRUGGLING! God has bound Himself to you by His Word and has sealed it with His oath. When you know that God has given you promises that cannot fail, you can have confidence that He will fulfill all that He promised. You pray without doubt!

Read this following passage of Scripture carefully:

Accordingly God also, in His desire to show more convincingly and beyond doubt to those who were to inherit the promise the unchangeableness of His purpose and plan, intervened (mediated) with an oath. This was so that, by two unchangeable things [His promise and His oath] in which it is impossible for God ever to prove false or deceive us, we who have fled [to Him] for refuge might have mighty indwelling strength and strong encouragement to grasp and hold fast the hope appointed for us and set before [us]. [Now] we have this [hope] as a sure and steadfast anchor of the soul [it cannot slip and cannot break down under whoever steps out upon it—a hope] that reaches and enters into [the very certainty of the Presence] within the veil. Where Jesus has entered in for us [in advance], a Forerunner having become a High Priest forever after the order (with the rank) of Melchizedek (Heb. 6:17-20, *AMP.*).

God has given you a mighty indwelling strength and strong encouragement that His promises cannot fail! He has given you an assurance that will not break down or crumble regardless of what you may face! When you *know* that you *know* that you *know* that you are living in a covenant relationship with God (who cannot fail, lie or deceive you) and you have Christ as your great High Priest, you will be able to pray with power and authority based on God's promises, and see them come to pass.

The strength of our position is in what we know!

You are an heir to all the promises of God! "And if ye be Christ's, then are ye Abraham's seed, and heirs according to the promise" (Gal. 3:29). "Now to Abraham and his seed were the promises made. He saith not, And to seeds, as of many; but as of one, And to thy seed, which is Christ" (Gal. 3:16).

The promises of God are safe. They are secured! They are sealed!

Every promise God has ever made to us is on the basis of Himself, His unfailing record! He has sealed every one of His promises, not just by Himself, but by His oath!

God is not a man that He should lie! It is impossible for God to lie. He has confirmed His promises to us by two unchangeable things:

1. His oath
2. His promise

God made a promise to Abraham that inclu[...] including you and me. He sealed it with His oath [...] no more doubt, no more fear, no more questio[...]

Paul said, "Men indeed swear by a greater [than themselves], and with them in all disputes the oath taken for confirmation is final [ending strife]" (Heb. 6:16, *AMP.*).

If this is true in the natural world, think about what it means in the spiritual realm. In essence, what Paul was saying is that every promise God gave us, every written promise He has sealed with His oath. This is final confirmation. It is *finished!*

God does not want just the standard of our natural minds or the world's standard to be the final word. He sealed His promises with His heavenly oath because He desires to show us more convincingly and beyond any doubt.

The same God who said, "Let there be light: and there was light" (Gen. 1:3), who created the world by the power of His word and who threw the sun, moon and stars into their orbits is speaking His eternal, never-failing words to us.

We can run to Him for refuge. He gives us proof! You will never have to be afraid! No more wavering! No more wondering if it is God's will! No more questioning! No more struggling!

When you come before the Father to intercede on behalf of your unsaved loved ones, family members and the unsaved in your city and on behalf of your nation, you can know *beyond any doubt* that He will hear and do "whatsoever you ask." Jesus said, "And whatsoever we ask, we receive of him, because we keep his commandments, and do those things that are pleasing in his sight" (1 John 3:22).

Every promise that God ever spoke to you through a dream, a word spoken by God or a prophecy through His written word will be fulfilled!

SPIRITUAL VISION!

The key to taking hold of these promises will be your ability to focus with spiritual vision.

When you develop spiritual vision and begin to pray, not according to what you see in the natural, but with your focus on God's promises, regardless of the circumstances, you will see the fulfillment of those promises!

We have allowed Satan to keep the blessings of God from us because we have succumbed to the spirits of intimidation. There has been an entire theology that has risen in this hour and caused the Body of Christ to shrink back from signs, wonders, the gifts of healing and the manifestation of the Holy Ghost.

God said it is time for you to stop being intimidated by the power of the enemy, and stop letting him rob you of the blessings that God has promised for you! Satan has succeeded in distracting the Body of Christ, but you will not be distracted any longer! You will keep your spiritual focus. You will not succumb to any negativism.

Stake out your territory!
When you do, know that Satan has
no right inside your territory!
KEEP HIM OUT!

The twin monsters of fear and doubt will be crushed under the heel of He who scarred the face of the devil two thousand years ago, when he tried to grab hold of Him as He was being resurrected! "And I will put enmity between thee and the woman, and between thy seed and her seed; it shall bruise thy head, and thou shalt bruise his heel" (Gen. 3:15).

It is time for you to stake out your spiritual territory. You must set your spiritual boundaries and then let the devil know that it belongs to God. The devil cannot enter your territory and he cannot have control!

This is God's time.

- He will use *you* to release salvation.
- He will use *you* to release healing.
- He will use *you* to release deliverance.
- He will use *you* to release miracles, signs and wonders!
- Stake out your territory!
- Set up your boundaries!

God told me to tell you, "Every prayer that you have ever prayed in your entire life is before Him right now. Not one of your prayers has been lost. You may have forgotten those prayers, but God said, 'Tell My people, I have not forgotten one.' There is nothing that God starts that He doesn't finish."

Many Christians have allowed Satan to invade their territory. Have you? Stake your claim! When you do, know that Satan has no right inside your territory. It is your ground. Don't let him deceive you! The earth is the Lord's and the fullness thereof.

Every unanswered prayer is not between you and the devil. Don't let the devil intimidate you. Every unanswered prayer is between *you* and *God*. It was God who made the promise, and when you pray according to the promises of God it has nothing to do with the devil.

Don't let him intimidate you!

It's your territory! It's not his! *Keep him out!*

If you have an unanswered prayer—go to God! If there is something you have asked God to do and it hasn't taken place, don't fight and argue and wrestle with the devil over it—it's none of his business! *It's between you and God!*

What are the unanswered prayers in your life? God has not forgotten the prayers you have prayed for the salvation of your loved ones. He has not forgotten the hours you have spent in prayer for the healing of your body or the financial breakthrough you need. This is God's time for you to stake your claim, cast off the spirits of doubt and fear and take hold of the answers you need. Receive this prophetic word into your spirit and act on it!

Your Prayers Must Be Divinely Energized!

Moses was considered the friend of God. That is the kind of relationship that Jesus talked about when He said, "Ye are my friends, if ye do whatsoever I command you. Henceforth I call you not servants; for the servant knoweth not what his lord doeth: but I have called you friends for all things that I have heard of my Father I have made known unto you" (John 15:14).

As we remain in continual communion and fellowship with Christ and walk in obedience to Him and His Word, we can know He always hears us. God hears even our faintest cry and will answer.

Just as God acted in response to Moses' intercession, spared Israel and extended His forgiveness to them, God will use your intercession as a means of releasing a wave of salvation, healing and deliverance, and entire cities and nations will be saved. Do you believe it? Do you see this new position of power and authority in your prayers that God wants you to take?

Jesus said, "Behold! I have given you authority and power to trample upon serpents and scorpions, and [physical and mental strength and ability] over all the power that the enemy [possesses]; and nothing shall in any way harm you" (Luke 10:19, *AMP.*).

The key to praying with power and receiving answers to your prayers lies in your relationship with the Lord. The greatest desire of the apostle Paul's heart was, "That I may know him, and the power of his resurrection, and the fellowship of his sufferings, being made conformable unto his death" (Phil. 3:10).

From your innermost being there must also arise an insatiable desire to know Christ in His fullness. With every fiber of your being you must cry out, *That I may know you!* You must be willing to shut yourself in with Him and spend time in His presence getting to know Him, allowing His words to take root in your heart. You must so desire and depend on His presence that you, too, will say, "If Your presence doesn't go with me, I don't want to go!" (see Exod. 33:15).

When you live in this intimate relationship, your prayers will be based on His desires and His will. You will no longer depend on your own natural understanding to pray. You will pray according to how He directs you by His Spirit working and living within you. Your prayers will be divinely energized.

Christ wants us to desire and hunger for Him above all else. He wants us to seek Him for who He is. And as we know Him intimately, His very life is imparted to us and we are transformed! This was the plan of Jehovah God when He gave birth to the Church 2,000 years ago. "Christ in you," Paul cried, "the hope of glory" (Col. 1:27).

Without this deep, intimate communion and relationship with Christ we are powerless and our prayers for others are just empty words. First and foremost in our prayers we must spend time shut in with the Father, waiting before Him in His presence, seeking His direction, drawing from His strength, allowing Him to reveal Himself to us.

Once we have entered into this place of communion and fellowship with God, we enter into *power intimacy* where we are positioned to intercede on behalf of our loved ones and for the lost, for our cities, for the 10/40 Window, for the unreached people groups, for the Muslim world, for the Hindu, the Buddhist, the devil worshipers, and for the last closed doors to the gospel. These doors will open! All from a new position of *power intimacy!*

CHRIST SPOKE THE PRAYER COMMAND AND IT WAS DONE!

Christ had a strong, powerful, intimate relationship with His Father. He spent many hours in prayer, alone with Him.

Jesus said, "I and my Father are one" (John 10:30). He told His disciples, "The words that I speak unto you I speak not of myself: but the Father that dwelleth in me, he doeth the works" (John 14:10). He was saying, "It's the Father living, dwelling, remaining and manifesting His power through Me."

No greater sermon on prayer can ever be preached than what Christ revealed through His example and life of prayer. Prayer was as natural to Him as breathing. He loved to pray. Christ taught the importance of intimacy in prayer, shutting out all distractions and getting alone with the Father. He said, "But when you pray, go into your [most] private room, and, closing the door, pray to your Father, Who is in secret; and your Father, Who sees in secret, will reward you in the open" (Matt. 6:6, AMP.). Often He would go to the Mount of Olives to pray. There were times when Jesus spent the entire night in prayer.

Before Christ began His ministry, He was led *by the Spirit* into the wilderness where He spent forty days and nights in prayer and fasting. During that time, He communed with the Father in preparation for the work He had been sent to fulfill. There, in the wilderness, in the power of the Spirit, He faced and defeated Satan.

At the Jordan River when He was baptized in water and was filled with the Holy Spirit, He prayed. "Now when all the people were baptized, it came to pass, that Jesus also being baptized, *and praying,* the heaven was opened" (Luke 3:21, emphasis added).

There were times after He had ministered to the needs of the masses that He felt the need to be alone with the Father in prayer. "But so much the more went there a fame abroad of him: and great multitudes came together to hear, and to be healed by him of their infirmities. *And he withdrew himself into the wilderness, and prayed*" (Luke 5:15,16, emphasis added).

Before He chose His twelve disciples, Christ spent the entire night in prayer. "And it came to pass in those days, that he went out into a mountain to pray and *continued all night in prayer* to God" (Luke 6:12, emphasis added).

As He prayed on the mountain with Peter, James and John, His entire countenance changed. As He communed with the Father, the glory of God emanated and radiated from His countenance. "And *as he prayed,* the fashion of his countenance was altered, and his raiment was white and glistening" (Luke 9:29, emphasis added).

Through prayer, the power of God was released. Whatever Christ spoke came to pass. He spoke to the impossible circumstances in people's lives and they were changed, healed, delivered and set free! It was not necessary to pray a long prayer pleading and begging the Father to heal or set people free from the bondage of Satan. Jesus knew God's will and He gave a *prayer command* based upon God's will and it was done!

To the leper, Jesus gave the prayer command to be "clean" and immediately, he was cleansed and made whole (see Matt. 8:1-4). To the man at the pool of Bethesda who had been paralyzed 38 years, Jesus spoke the prayer command, "Rise, take up thy bed, and walk" (John 5:8) and immediately the man arose from his bed and walked (see John 5:1-16). To the woman with a spirit of infirmity who was bowed over for 18 years, Jesus spoke the prayer command, "Woman, thou art loosed from thine infirmity" (Luke 13:12). He laid His hands on her and immediately she was made straight (see Luke 13:11-13).

The miracle power of God was released into these impossible situations as Christ spoke because He had first won the victories in prayer.

WHAT WAS THE SECRET TO THE POWER BEHIND CHRIST'S WORDS?

The great victories Jesus experienced as He ministered to the needs of the people—opening blind eyes, unstopping deaf ears, healing all manner of diseases, raising the dead—were not automatic. Although He was the Son of God, Jesus did not win these victories in His own strength. He had stripped Himself of His divine abilities and was subject to the same human limitations as you and I. "Who, being in very nature God, did not consider equality with God something to be grasped, but made himself nothing, taking the very nature of a servant, being made in human likeness" (Phil. 2:6,7, *NIV*).

He did absolutely nothing independent of the Father. Everything He did was a result of what the Father had revealed to Him, while He was in His Presence *in prayer.*

Not once among the people did Jesus *pray* for the sick! He did not once ask the Father to heal anyone. He spent time alone in prayer; but when He ministered to the needs of the people, He spoke with power and authority and the work was accomplished. Knowing it was His Father's will to heal the sick, He spoke the *prayer command* and it was done!

Christ had a strong relationship with the Father through prayer. He knew Him intimately and knew that whenever He prayed the Father would *always* hear and answer. There was absolutely no trace of doubt the Father would do whatever He asked.

When Jesus stood at the hillside outside Lazarus's tomb, He was surrounded by unbelief. The Jews were full of unbelief. They said, "Could not this man, which opened the eyes of the blind, have caused that even this man should not have died?" (John 11:37). Even Mary and Martha were not expecting Him to raise Lazarus from the dead. Their eyes were still on the natural circumstances. When Jesus told them to roll away the stone, Martha told Him, "By this time he stinketh: for he hath been dead four days" (v. 39).

Picture this: They rolled the stone away and Jesus is standing outside the cave. Inside the tomb is the cold, lifeless body of Lazarus wrapped in grave clothes. Jesus lifts His eyes toward heaven and prays, "Father, I thank thee that thou hast heard me. And I knew that thou hearest me always: but because of the people which stand by I said it, that they may believe that thou hast sent me" (John 11:41,42).

CHRIST'S EXAMPLE IN PRAYER: TOTAL CONFIDENCE!

In this brief prayer, we see the total confidence Jesus had in His relationship with the Father. Even before He prayed, He knew the Father would hear and answer Him; He said, "I *know* that You always hear Me" (John 11:42, *NKJV*). When you pray, do you pray with this same total confidence, knowing God always hears and will do as He promised?

Based on this knowing and the strength of His relationship, Jesus gave the prayer command of faith. With a loud voice, He cried out, "Lazarus, come forth!" (John 11:43).

As He spoke, the cold, dark cave was invaded with the life stream of almighty God. Like a bolt of lightning, the life flow of

God hit Lazarus's cold, lifeless, stinking body. When God's power struck, he stood up and walked out of the cave still wearing his grave clothes!

Christ intends you to have this same powerful intimacy with Him through prayer whereby you know, beyond any doubt, that He always hears and will answer your prayers!

In His great high priestly prayer for the Church, Christ prayed, "That they all may be one; as thou, Father, art in me, and I in thee, that they may also be one in us: that the world may believe that thou hast sent me" (John 17:21). The same powerful relationship Christ has with the Father, where they are united together as One, He desires for us to have with Him, and He has made it possible.

In His final moments with His disciples, before going to the cross, Jesus said, "Dwell in Me, and I will dwell in you. [Live in Me, and I will live in you.] Just as no branch can bear fruit of itself without abiding in (being vitally united to) the vine, neither can you bear fruit unless you abide in Me" (John 15:4, *AMP.*).

This is the key to having Christ's power flowing continually through your life, enabling you to pray from a position of power and authority.

POWER INTIMACY THROUGH PRAYER IS THE KEY!

Unbroken fellowship and communion with Christ and the Father through the Holy Spirit releases His power to produce fruit—to heal the sick, cast out devils and raise the dead!

Jesus said, "If you live in Me [abide vitally united to Me] and My words remain in you and continue to live in your hearts, ask whatever you will and it shall be done for you. When you bear (produce) much fruit, My Father is honored and glorified, and you show and prove yourselves to be true followers of Mine" (John 15:7,8, *AMP.*).

Christ has planned for you to bear much fruit! He has planned for you to receive whatever you ask, as you abide in Him and He in you! When God's power flows through you to bring healing and deliverance to the world, it brings glory to Him!

Beloved, it is impossible for you to pray in the dimension of power and authority God intends in this power-intimacy hour unless you *first* come into this strong, intimate relationship with Christ. Without it, there can be no real power and no fruit in your life; without this intimate relationship, your prayers are ineffective and void of power!

The key to asking in prayer and receiving whatever you ask lies *in your relationship with Christ.* The word "abide" used in the *King James Version* means to remain virtually united. In this scripture, it is referring to a relationship with Christ whereby we remain in Him and live in unbroken fellowship and communion with Him.

The reason we have not been able to demonstrate the reality of the power of the gospel to a lost and dying world is because we moved away from our position of intimacy a long time ago, or we never really matured spiritually to the place where we are truly one with Christ.

Christ's purpose and intention for His Church is that we be the most powerful force on the earth! His purpose is that His life, His unlimited power and His glory flow through us unhindered! His purpose for your life is that this same power and anointing that is in Him flow through you to bring salvation, healing and deliverance to those around you! As Paul wrote, Christ is now seated,

Far above all principality, and power, and might, and dominion, and every name that is named, not only in this world, but also in that which is to come (Eph. 1:21).

Jesus said,

> You have not chosen Me, but I have chosen you and
> I have appointed you [I have planted you], that you might
> go and bear fruit and keep on bearing, and that your
> fruit may be lasting [that it may remain, abide], so that
> whatever you ask the Father in My Name [as presenting
> all that I AM], He may give it to you (John 15:16, *AMP.*).

Christ intends that there will be a continual flow of His
unlimited power that will continually produce and bear spiritual
fruit in your life. He hasn't planned for there to ever be a time in
your life when you are barren or unfruitful. If you are barren, it is
because you have somehow become cut off from the life flow that is
in Christ. Perhaps you need to renew that intimate union with Him.

Christ said you must have an intimate relationship (be vitally
united with Him as one) where His life and power flow continually through you. Jesus said, "I am the Vine; you are the branches.
Whoever lives in Me and I in him bears much (abundant) fruit.
However, apart from Me [cut off from vital union with Me] you
can do nothing" (John 15:5, *AMP.*).

In the natural realm, the branch does not struggle to produce
fruit. The fruit of the vine comes as the result of the life of the
vine flowing through the branch. God never intended for you to
struggle to produce spiritual fruit. He never intended for you to
struggle to produce faith or any of the gifts or manifestations of
His Spirit. Neither does He intend for you to struggle to pray
with power and authority. As long as you live in this intimate
relationship with Christ, where you are drawing your life from
Him and His words remain in you, His life will flow through
you. The power and authority that is in Him will pour through
you as you pray.

This is a day-by-day, moment-by-moment relationship where His Spirit is working to produce His life in you. Christ has planned for you to produce much fruit! He has planned for you to continually produce fruit! He has planned for your fruit to remain!

The great problem we face within the Church is that we have moved away from an intimate relationship with Christ where we draw our very life from Him. Instead of having this intimate relationship with Him, we have become self-sufficient and self-absorbed in our own needs and desires. We have relied on and trusted in our own human efforts to fulfill the work He has called us to do.

As a result, we are like branches that are cut off from their life source, and we are dead—dried up on the vine! The reason many of our pulpits are so powerless is because pastors, evangelists, ministers and teachers are cut off from the real life flow of God's power because of their prayerlessness. Instead of coming to the pulpit fresh from the altar and presence of God, they come in their own strength.

> *Some Christians have become impotent—powerless! Jesus said we cannot produce fruit unless we remain in Him.*

The Church today is filled with Christians who have become so involved, so busy with their own needs and desires, so caught up with their works, the work of God and their ministries, they have failed to maintain an intimate relationship with Christ through prayer. They have become impotent—powerless! Jesus said we cannot produce fruit unless we remain in Him!

HAVE YOU ABANDONED YOUR FIRST LOVE?

In His letter to the seven churches, Christ reproved the church in Ephesus because the believers had lost their place of intimacy with Him. He told them, "I know your works. I know your hard work, your perseverance and all the things you have done for Me and for the sake of the Gospel. You have endured many hardships for Me."

These Ephesian believers were so busy doing the work of the Lord, they failed in the one area most vital to Him. Jesus told them, "But I have this [one charge to make] against you: that you have left (abandoned) the love that you had at first [you have deserted Me, your first love]" (Rev. 2:4, *AMP.*).

Christ did not say they had forgotten their first love, or that they had lost it, but they had left it. It was not that they no longer had any love for their Lord. They still loved Him, but the fervency and intensity of their first (or bridal) love was no longer there.

They had continued with their good works, but the works they did were no longer motivated and fueled by their love for Christ. This was not a light offense in the eyes of the Lord. He warned them that unless they repented and turned back to their first love, His judgment would come swiftly upon them, and He would remove this church from its position of influence and it would eventually cease to exist.

The call of the Spirit today is, first of all, a call to the Church of Jesus Christ to return to a personal, intimate relationship with Christ *through prayer*. We will be barren, cut off from the divine life flow of God, without a renewed dedication and commitment to this intimacy with Him through prayer.

The key to the release of God's power flowing through the apostle Paul was his intimate relationship with Christ. God's power was so manifested through him that when people took handkerchiefs that had been placed on his body and placed them on the sick, they were healed and demons were cast out. "And God wrought special miracles by the hands of Paul: so that from his body were brought unto the sick handkerchiefs or aprons, and the diseases departed from them, and the evil spirits went out of them" (Acts 19:11,12).

The life of God flowed out of Paul, not because of who Paul was or because of his righteousness, but because he had an intimate relationship with Christ where he had become *one with Him*. Paul knew he was in Christ and Christ lived within him. Paul could say, "I am crucified with Christ: nevertheless I live; yet not I, but Christ liveth in me: and the life which I now live in the flesh I live by the faith of the Son of God, who loved me, and gave himself for me" (Gal. 2:20).

Paul was saying, "It's no longer me; it is Christ living His life in and through me. He lives and remains in me. I am virtually united to Him and He lives and remains in me. It's Christ's life, His words, His power, His works!"

POWER INTIMACY!

In your relationship with Christ, can you say, *It is no longer my life, my will, my desires, but Christ who lives His life in me? I am one with Christ, He lives and remains in me, and I live and remain in Him?*

From the innermost depths of his being, Paul cried, *That I may know Him!*

[For my determined purpose is] that I may know Him [that I may progressively become more deeply and intimately acquainted with Him, perceiving and recognizing and understanding the wonders of His Person more strongly and more clearly], and that I may in that same way come to know the power outflowing from His resurrection [which it exerts over believers], and that I may so share His sufferings as to be continually transformed [in spirit into His likeness even] to His death (Phil. 3:10, *AMP.*).

Is this the cry and longing of your heart? Don't seek after things. Don't seek His power. Don't seek His gifts. Don't seek manifestations. Become consumed with a desire to know Christ intimately and live in unbroken communion and fellowship with Him. Then, when you come into this powerful position in Christ, you will be able to pray with power and authority and take dominion in the spirit realm.

This, beloved, is where we must begin if we are to truly know the power of prayer and be used by God to impact the world through our prayers!

ONLY ONE THING IS NEEDED!

One day the Lord was in the home of Martha and Mary. Martha was preoccupied with ministering to His needs and those of her household. All her attention had become focused upon the necessary preparations and work that had to be done. "But Martha was cumbered about much serving" (Luke 10:40). The word "cumbered" in this verse means distracted. Jesus, the Son of God, the Savior of the world, the giver of life, was in her home, but she had become distracted by all the preparations.

On the other hand, Mary had positioned herself at the feet of Jesus. "As Jesus and his disciples were on their way, he came to a village where a woman named Martha opened her home to him. She had a sister called Mary, who sat at the Lord's feet listening to what he said" (Luke 10:38,39, *NIV*).

Mary was consumed with her desire to be in the Lord's presence. She sat at His feet with her eyes fixed intently upon Him. She shut out everything else—the hustle and bustle around her, the demands of the hour, the angry glances of her sister. Nothing else mattered to her at that moment. She had lost all track of time and space as she sat there with all her energies focused on Christ and the words of life He was speaking.

When Martha complained to Jesus and asked Him to tell Mary to help her, He answered: "You are worried and upset about many things, *but only one thing is needed.* Mary has chosen what is better, and it will not be taken away from her" (Luke 10:41,42, *NIV,* emphasis added).

The Church today is like Martha. The great majority of Christians, including ministers and leaders, have become so preoccupied with other things in their busyness for the Lord (themselves, problems, work of the ministry), they have become distracted and have neglected the most important part.

Jesus said *only one thing is needed.*

We have become so caught up in our good works that we have failed to spend time alone, shut in with Christ in intimate fellowship and communion. The one thing we need above everything else is intimacy with Christ where we have shut out the demands and needs of the hour and have given ourselves in total abandonment to Him. Sitting at His feet and in His Presence is where His power is released within us.

PURSUE CHRIST WITH PASSIONATE DESIRE!

Are you ready to move to a higher level of prayer into a stronger, more intimate communion with Christ where you are abiding in Him and His Word is abiding in you?

This is the only way you will be able to pray with the power and authority God intends you to have to change the spiritual atmosphere in your home, impact your city and help change the spiritual destiny of nations.

I challenge you to pursue Christ with passionate desire. Make Him your number-one desire—not your family, not your career, not your goals and plans, not even your ministry or work for Him. Rekindle the fires of your first love where you are continually longing to know Christ in His fullness.

Christ wants you to know Him, not just have knowledge gained by hearing or reading about Him. Not a theory. Not head knowledge. He wants to reveal Himself to you through direct intimate communion with Him. You need to know Christ as He is today, not according to the limited understanding of your natural mind, but according to a personal revelation by the Holy Spirit.

David cried out to God with passionate desire, "O God, thou art my God; early will I seek thee...my flesh longeth for thee in a dry and thirsty land, where no water is" (Ps. 63:1). Make this the prayer of your heart! David said, "My whole being follows hard after You and clings closely to You" (Ps. 63:8, *AMP.*). Does your entire being cry out for Christ?

From the innermost depths of his being, Paul cried out, *That I may know Him!* Be consumed with a desire and longing after Christ; with your entire being— spirit, soul, body—pursue Him. Shut out all distractions and get alone with Him in prayer.

David said, "My soul, wait thou only upon God; for my expectation is from him. He only is my rock and my salvation: he is my defence; I shall not be moved" (Ps. 62:5,6).

When you *wait* for the Lord in prayer, it is not a passive action. The word "wait" in the Scripture means to remain in readiness or expectation. After we pour our hearts out to the Lord, we are to wait, to act in faith, and remain in a state of expectancy, knowing He will make us victorious.

When you truly learn how to wait for the Lord in prayer, you will be immovable! Instead of expecting your help to come from natural sources, your spiritual vision will be focused! Your hope, your expectation and your confidence will be fixed on Him and His promises, and you will not be fearful regardless of what you face.

As you wait for the Lord in prayer, you come into an intimacy with Him where you are able to hear His voice. He opens His heart to you and reveals His will and plan for your life. He gives you discernment to know what actions to take to be victorious in every circumstance and battle you face.

When you wait before Him, He reveals His timing, and positions you for victory. Then as you pray according to what He has shown you and whispered to you during your time of intimacy with Him, you are able to take the victory you need in your life—in your physical body, in your finances, in your family and in your ministry.

Beloved,

I pray right now that Christ will bring you into an intimacy with Him far greater than anything you have ever dreamed possible! I pray that God will release into your life an unquenchable spiritual hunger and thirst that will cause you to seek Him with all your heart and soul. And, as you learn to wait before Him in prayer, I pray He will reveal Himself to you in His fullness. I pray that you will come into a new intimacy with Christ where you hear His voice, and that your spiritual focus will be fixed on Him and Him alone.

I pray that you will enter into an experience where you are truly one with Christ, where you know, beyond any doubt, that you are in Him and He is in you!

I pray, as you enter into a new position of power intimacy, you will begin to pray in the same power and authority that Christ prayed. As Christ's life flows through you like a mighty river, I pray God will use you to pray prayers that will release God's power to manifest miracles of salvation, healing and deliverance in Jesus' name!

CHAPTER 5

DO AS YOU HAVE SAID!

Are you ready to move into this powerful new dimension of prayer and authority Jesus taught where whatsoever you ask you will receive? There is only one way to obtain this power in prayer.

Look at John 15:7 in *The Amplified Bible*. Jesus said, "If you live in Me [abide vitally united to Me] and My words remain in you and continue to live in your hearts, ask whatever you will, and it shall be done for you." Only as you abide in Him and allow His Word to live and remain and work in you, do you obtain this position of power in prayer where you will be able to ask *whatsoever* and it will be done.

Christ and the Word are inseparable. He is the living Word. "In the beginning was the Word, and the Word was with God, and the Word was God. The same was in the beginning with God. All things were made by him; and without him was not any thing made that was made" (John 1:1-3). To have the Word abiding in you means more than simply reading or hearing the Word. The type of "abiding" to which I am referring is the Word that does not depart from your mind. It penetrates your mind and spirit.

As the Word takes root in your spirit, your mind is renewed. Your spiritual eyes are opened. You will know Him. You will see clearly what He has planned for you and see the things He has prepared for you. When the Word, the written and living Word, abides in you, the promises of God will come alive within you. When you face a circumstance or problem, you will not wonder if it is God's will or wonder if God will meet your need; you will know His will and you will pray His promises according to His will! Throughout this relationship where you abide in Christ, you must continually draw from His strength.

Jesus lived His life on earth by the Father who sent Him. Jesus' words, His actions and His works were all a result of the Father living in Him.

- And he that sent me is with me: the Father hath not left me alone (John 8:29).
- The Father is in me, and I in him (John 10:38).
- Believest thou not that I am in the Father, and the Father in me? (John 14:10).
- The Son can do nothing of himself, but what he seeth the Father do: for what things soever he doeth, these also doeth the Son likewise. For the Father loveth the Son, and showeth him all things that himself doeth (John 5:19,20).

In Christ dwells all the fullness of the Godhead. Therefore, when you are "abiding" in Christ, the Godhead—Father, Son and Holy Spirit—dwells in you!

For in Him the whole fullness of Deity (the Godhead) continues to dwell in bodily form [giving complete expression of the divine nature]. And you are in Him, made full and having come to fullness of life [in Christ you too are filled with the Godhead—Father, Son and Holy Spirit—and reach full spiritual stature]. And He is the Head of all rule and authority (Col. 2:9,10, *AMP.*).

At this very moment, Jesus is seated at the right hand of the Father. He has been exalted and given a name above every name. He has the supreme place of power and authority in the universe. And you are seated with Him! (See Eph. 2:6.)

 Your position in Christ gives you dominion, power, authority and might to pray bold prophetic prayers!

In this position of dominion, power, authority and strength you are able to ask whatsoever you will and it shall be done! You are able to pray bold, prophetic prayers because you are in an intimate relationship, abiding in Christ who is seated on the throne!

WE MUST PRAY PRAYERS FROM THE THRONE ROOM!

In this place of dominion with Christ, you pray prayers from the throne room that enforce God's will on the earth. The words that you speak are directed by the Holy Spirit and activate the power of God to bring what you speak to pass. From this position of abiding in Christ, you are able to go boldly before the Father to present His promises and *ask* based on what He has promised. Christ has promised that whatsoever you ask you will receive. Jesus said:

> You have not chosen Me, but I have chosen you and I have appointed you [I have planted you], that you might go and bear fruit and keep on bearing, and that your fruit may be lasting [that it may remain, abide], so that whatever you ask the Father in My Name [as presenting all that I AM], He may give it to you (John 15:16, *AMP.*).

The word "ask" in this verse in the original Greek means a demand of something due. This does not mean that we are to go around demanding and ordering God to do whatever we please. In Jesus' name we are to make a demander request—what legally belongs to us as a result of the victory Christ has already won.

Praying in the name of Jesus is more than simply repeating the words, "in the name of Jesus." All that Jesus is and all the power and authority He possesses is in His name! All the fullness of the Godhead is in His name!

- There is salvation in His name!
- There is healing in His name!
- There is creative power in His name!
- There is deliverance in His name!
- Everything you need is in His name!

In the power and authority of His name, we have everything we need to drive the forces of Satan out of our homes, cities and the nations of the world. We have been appointed as Christ's legal representatives on this earth and have legal power and authority to use His name. In Jesus' name, we have been given full power and authority to act on His behalf in the same manner He would if He were living and walking on this earth.

From our position of dominion, power, authority and might with Christ, seated on the throne, we can go boldly before the Father and ask—make a demand on what God has promised—in the power and authority of Jesus' name and it will be done! When we pray from this position of dominion with Christ, we can take God's promises to Him and say, "Do as you have said." It is like going to the bank, presenting a check and drawing money out of your account.

This is the type of powerful prayer David prayed to God regarding His promise that He would establish David's house on the throne of Israel forever. David's entire prayer is recorded in 2 Samuel 7:18-29. Take time to read it in its entirety. Within this prayer, David makes a demand on the promise God gave him.

After God gave him this promise, through Nathan, the prophet, David went before the Lord. Listen to his prayer:

Who am I, O Lord God? and what is my house, that thou hast brought me hitherto? And this was yet a small thing in thy sight, O Lord God; but thou hast spoken also of thy servant's house for a great while to come....Wherefore thou art great, O Lord God: for there is none like thee, neither is there any God beside thee, according to all that we have heard with our ears (2 Sam. 7:18,19,22).

Then David spread God's promise out before Him and made a demand on that promise. David came boldly before God because he knew God's faithfulness and that His promises would not fail. He said:

And now, O Lord God, the word that thou hast spoken concerning thy servant, and concerning his house, establish it for ever, and do *as thou has said.* And now, O Lord God, thou art that God, and thy words be true, and thou hast promised this goodness unto thy servant: Therefore now let it please thee to bless the house of thy servant, that it may continue for ever before thee: for thou, O Lord God, hast spoken it (2 Sam. 7:25,28,29, emphasis added).

> *Knowing that His promises cannot fail, we are to come boldly before God, spread out His promises and say, "Do as You have said!"*

This is the same basis on which God expects us to come to Him regarding His promises to us. Knowing that His promises cannot fail, we are to come boldly before Him, spread out His promises and say, "Do as You have said!"

GOD IS SAYING TO YOU, "ASK!"

God is ready to act on your behalf! He has given you His promises and bound Himself to you with His oath and His Word. He has made full provision to meet every need.

He has given you the power and authority to fulfill His will in the nations of the world. He has called, anointed and commissioned you to heal the sick, cast out devils and proclaim the gospel to the nations in a demonstration of His power. He is now waiting for you to ask—to make a demand on what He has already provided through Christ.

What would you do if God appeared to you and said, "Ask what I shall give thee"? (1 Kings 3:5). That is what He said to Solomon. And that is what He is saying to you by His Spirit today. He is waiting for you to *ask!*

God spoke through Isaiah, "Ask me of things to come concerning my sons, and concerning the work of my hands command ye me" (Isa. 45:11). In this end-time hour, God is pouring out His anointing to bring us into a new dimension of dominion, power, authority and strength in our prayers where we are boldly presenting His promises and making a demand on all He has given us.

God is saying to you, "*Ask*—ask what I shall give you!"

There is no limit to what God will do through Christ today as we begin to pray with new revelation, boldness and authority to fulfill His will on the earth. He has promised, "Ask of me, and I shall give thee the heathen for thine inheritance, and the uttermost parts of the earth for thy possession" (Ps. 2:8).

The time has come when we must pray from our position of dominion, authority and might with Christ in the heavenlies on behalf of the nations that are still closed to the gospel. We need to come before God on behalf of Egypt, Saudi Arabia, Syria, Iran, Iraq, Turkey, China, Indonesia, North Korea, Thailand and the countries in the 10/40 Window and *ask*—make a demand on God's promises.

Knowing that He has called, anointed and commissioned us to take the gospel to the ends of the earth, we must boldly go before Him and in the name of Jesus command the powers of darkness to leave. We must go deep into the Spirit, bind the spirits that are exerting dominion over these countries and command them to leave in Jesus' name. We must go into battle through this new end-time prophetic prayer anointing God is releasing and destroy the Muslim, Buddhist and Hindu strongholds and all forms of idolatry and religious spirits that are holding people in bondage.

Dr. C. Peter Wagner has written a dynamic, revolutionary booklet, *Confronting the Queen of Heaven*, that exposes one of the most prominent, demonic principalities behind the various forms of idolatry in the world today. In his book, Peter traces this demonic principality back to the idolatry and worship of the goddess Diana and how it is directly linked with Islam. His book lays out a strategy that will unite Christians to confront and tear down the stronghold of the "Queen of Heaven" that has roots in the majority of the nations of the world. Every intercessor needs a copy of this strategic book.

From our position with Christ of dominion, power, authority and might, we must pray bold, prophetic prayers, knowing that Christ has said, "And this gospel of the kingdom shall be preached in all the world for a witness unto all nations; and then shall the end come" (Matt. 24:14).

We must begin to declare God's prophetic will:

- In the name of Jesus, we declare that Egypt, Saudi Arabia, Syria, Iran, Iraq, North Korea and China are no longer closed to the gospel!
- We declare in the name of Jesus that the Word of God will penetrate into every region in these countries.
- We declare in the name of Jesus that there will be a great end-time harvest of souls won into the kingdom of God!
- We declare every unlawful work of the enemy to be bound and cast out from its hiding place.
- We declare in the name of Jesus that a spirit of salvation, healing and deliverance will be loosed with signs,

miracles and wonders manifested as a witness that Jesus is who He claims to be—the Son of the living God.

• We declare that the name of Jesus will be lifted up and that God's power and glory will cover these nations as a witness to the world of His almighty power!

God is waiting for you to *ask*. He has promised that "Before they call, I will answer; and while they are yet speaking, I will hear" (Isa. 65:24). He is saying to you now, "Call unto me, and I will answer thee, and show thee great and mighty things, which thou knowest not" (Jer. 33:3).

Remember, God is going to bring us into a new dimension of authority in our prayers where our words, spoken with authority, invested in the promises of God, will enable us to confront every stronghold of the enemy!

Beloved,

I pray for you right now that God will release a spirit of revelation upon you. I pray that He will enable you to see the position of dominion, power, authority and might that He wants you to take with Christ in the heavenlies.

I pray that you will enter into this new dimension of power in prayer as you learn to abide in Christ and allow His Word to dwell and remain in you.

I pray that God will remove the veil from your eyes and that you will see Christ as your great High Priest, standing at the right hand of the Father to intercede for you.

I pray that God will reveal the power of His promises and His faithfulness to keep His promises to you.

I pray that this end-time prophetic prayer anointing will come upon you and cover you. I pray that you will live under this prayer anointing that you will pray as you rise every morning. I pray that during the day you will be surrounded by a prayer atmosphere and that before you sleep at night you will spend time alone with God.

As this prayer anointing comes upon you, I pray that you will pray bold, prophetic prayers based on what the Spirit has revealed to you.

I pray that God will release an anointing upon you to pray prayers that will release His power to work in your life, in your family, in your finances and in all your circumstances.

I pray that He will open your spiritual eyes to see His plan and purpose in this end-time hour, and that you will pray bold, prophetic prayers to destroy the strongholds of the enemy and bring in the harvest of the nations.

In Jesus' mighty name!

Amen!

CHAPTER

6

HOLY SPIRIT ENERGIZED PRAYERS

As God releases this end-time prophetic prayer anointing on the Church, He will bring us into a new dimension of power and authority that will enable us to spoil the devil's house!

Jesus said, "No man can enter into a strong man's house, and spoil his goods, except he will first bind the strong man; and then he will spoil his house" (Mark 3:27).

The word "spoil" in this verse is translated from the Greek word *diarpazo*, which means "to seize asunder, plunder." Now, look at this same verse in *The Amplified Bible*, which gives a clearer understanding of the original Greek.

But no one can go into a strong man's house and ransack his household goods right and left and seize them as plunder unless he first binds the strong man; then indeed he may [thoroughly] plunder his house (Mark 3:27, *AMP*.).

Through the power and authority of the Holy Spirit, not only will we bind the evil principalities that have gained strongholds in the nations, but we are also going to shake his kingdom, pull down his strongholds and seize from his hands the spiritual territory that belongs to the kingdom of God!

The way we will be able to move into this new dimension of power and authority, which will literally shake Satan's kingdoms and destroy his last remaining strongholds in the nations, is through a fresh revelation and release of the Holy Spirit to pray through us.

One of the major reasons the prayers of the Church have not yet impacted the nations to the degree God intended is because the great majority of Christians in our churches have not fully understood or recognized the awesome, unlimited power God has made available to us through prayer. The average Christian has not only had a very limited knowledge regarding the power of prayer and the position of power and authority God has given the Church through prayer, but their experience in prayer has been limited!

The average Christian has not assumed his or her responsibility in prayer for their families, cities and nations. It has only been in the last few years that the Church has begun to recognize the importance of spiritual warfare and intercession and to unite as a powerful force to cover the nations in prayer.

We are now seeing the greatest prayer movement in the history of the Church. God has raised up anointed, powerful ministers such as Dr. C. Peter Wagner with the Spiritual Warfare Network of the A.D. 2000 and Beyond Movement; Cindy Jacobs with Generals of Intercession; Dick Eastman with Every Home For Christ; Pastor Ted Haggard and Beverly Peques with the Christian Information Network; Dr. Bill Bright with Campus Crusade for Christ; and hundreds of other prayer ministries worldwide.

This is not the work of a man or an organization. God has raised up these ministries to teach and lead the Body of Christ into a greater awareness regarding the power of prayer and a better understanding regarding spiritual warfare. There are now an estimated 180 million people worldwide who have made a commitment to pray for the spreading of the gospel to the nations of the world before the end of the year 2000!

As the Church mobilizes and unites in prayer, our effectiveness in fulfilling God's end-time purpose and plan, in destroying the enemy's strongholds, in opening doors now closed to the gospel, and establishing the kingdom of God in the nations will be determined according to the proportion we are empowered and directed by the Holy Spirit in our prayers.

TOTAL DEPENDENCE ON THE HOLY SPIRIT TO EMPOWER OUR PRAYERS!

We cannot rely on our natural resources and our own understanding. We must break through all natural abilities, cast aside our self-reliance and fight spiritual warfare in His power!

The apostle Paul told the Ephesians, "Be strong in the Lord, and in the power of his might" (Eph. 6:10). How is it possible for us to do this? Paul continued by instructing the Ephesians to put on the whole armor of God, which would enable them to stand against all the strategies and tricks of the devil and also to defeat him and "quench all the fiery darts of the wicked" (6:16).

Then Paul gave them the key to walking in the power of God's might. He explained, "Praying always with all prayer and supplication in the Spirit, and watching thereunto with all perseverance and supplication for all saints" (Eph. 6:18).

We are to pray always with all types of prayer *in the spirit!* We cannot afford to lean our own natural understanding to pray prayers to break the strongholds of the enemy affecting our homes and our families and destroying our cities and nations.

Our prayers must be directed by the Holy Spirit, divinely energized, and empowered by the Holy Spirit! God wants you to be so full of the Holy Spirit and yielded to Him that the Holy Spirit will pray prayers through you that are directed and empowered by God to pierce through the spiritual forces of darkness and destroy the enemy strongholds.

Prayers that are prayed only in our limited natural strength cannot get the job done. Weak, ineffective, timid prayers will not get the job done! Don't think for a moment that the spiritual forces of darkness keeping untold thousands in your city in bondage to drugs, alcohol, sexual perversion, lust, greed and every other form of sin will loose their hold according to prayers that are prayed in man's natural strength.

We must have a total dependence on the Holy Spirit within us to empower our prayers. Too many times when Christians pray, they are depending on their own intelligence, their knowledge of the Word or the strength of their faith alone. The battle must be fought and won in the power and anointing of almighty God!

It doesn't matter how long, how smart, how loud or how hard you pray; if it is not done in the Spirit it will be ineffective and the enemy will not move one inch! Our prayers, when *energized by the Holy Spirit*, make things happen!

The emphasis in our prayers must be on the Spirit praying and interceding through us, not on ourselves. Forget your personality. It does not matter who you are or how strong or how weak and insignificant you may think you are. On the outside, you may look like a meek, mild gray-headed grandmother. You may be a conservative businessman or a young college student. However, if you are full of the Holy Spirit and yielded completely to Him, you can stand toe-to-toe with the enemy.

Through the power and anointing of the Holy Spirit, you are transformed into a mighty spiritual warrior. As He prays through you, the words coming out of your mouth are spoken in the power and authority of the Holy Spirit. Demons recognize the power and authority of Jesus' name and they must obey! Through the power of the Holy Spirit within you, demons are subject to you; when you pray in the Spirit, the demons obey.

Satan recognizes if we have a relationship with God. When you come face-to-face with demonic powers, if you don't have this experience you become vulnerable to his attacks. In the book of Acts we read about the seven sons of Sceva, a Jewish chief priest who tried to cast a demon out of a man. They tried casting the demon out in the name of Jesus, but the evil spirit recognized they did not have a real relationship with Christ.

These seven men said, "In the name of Jesus, whom Paul preaches, I command you to come out" (Acts 19:13, *NIV*). These men had heard about Jesus. They had undoubtedly heard Paul preach, heal the sick and cast out devils in Jesus' name. But they were not born-again sons of the living God. The words they spoke were powerless because the Holy Spirit was not living within them to give them the power and authority to overcome the demon principalities.

The evil spirit answered them, "Jesus I know, and I know about Paul, but who are you?" (Acts 19:15, *NIV*). Then the evil spirit that was in the man attacked them and overpowered them. The evil spirit gave them such a beating they ran out of the house naked and bleeding.

WE HAVE A DIVINE COMMUNICATION LINK!

God never intended you to face the power of the enemy in your own limited natural strength. *Never!*

When God gave birth to the Church 2,000 years ago, He never intended it to know any limits. He gave it divine capability to face all the power of the enemy in 100-percent victory, and to do the same works Jesus did in the same power and anointing.

Through the indwelling presence of the Holy Spirit, the third Person of the Trinity, you are no longer limited to praying in your natural understanding. The Holy Spirit has been given to you so that you will be able to pray Holy Spirit-energized prayers!

The apostle Paul understood our limited natural abilities. He recognized that we could not pray according to our natural, carnal minds. He said,

> But the natural man receiveth not the things of the Spirit of God: for they are foolishness unto him: neither can he know them, because they are spiritually discerned (1 Cor. 2:14).

Paul also said, "For we know not what we should pray for as we ought" (Rom. 8:26).

How many times have you faced problems, circumstances and situations where you just did not know how to pray? Have you ever faced circumstances that were so overwhelming, so unbearable, so intense or the need so great, you had no words? You could not speak and all that came out of your mouth was deep groanings?

It was not God's intention for His children to depend on their natural minds to communicate with Him. He gave us a divine capability, a direct line of communication, which no power can hinder or destroy. We have a divine link with the Father!

God sent a part of Himself, the third Person of the Trinity, to live within us to make intercession for us. By His Spirit, we are granted access to the Father. Paul said, "Ye have received the Spirit of adoption, whereby we cry, Abba, Father" (Rom. 8:15). It is the Holy Spirit within us who reveals the things God has prepared for us and the things He has freely given us.

> But as it is written, Eye hath not seen, nor ear heard, neither have entered into the heart of man, the things which God hath prepared for them that love him. But God hath revealed them unto us by his Spirit....Now we have received, not the spirit of the world, but the spirit which is of God; that we might know the things that are freely given to us of God (1 Cor. 2:9,10,12).

By His Spirit within us, we are able to pray in unknown tongues, which is a direct link to God that man does not understand and Satan and his demons cannot hinder! Paul shared, "For he that speaketh in an unknown tongue speaketh not unto men, but unto God: for no man understandeth him; howbeit in the spirit he speaketh mysteries" (1 Cor. 14:2).

▽ *We have a divine link with the Father!* ▽

There is an awesome power released as we pray in "unknown tongues." I pray in tongues regularly for hours at a time. As I pray, my spirit is praying directly to the heart of God. The Holy Spirit is empowering me and I know things are changing in the spirit realm. Hindrances are being removed! Demons are being bound! The power of God is being released and the will of God is being accomplished!

How do I know this? Because the Holy Spirit within me is making intercession before the Father according to His will!

DIVINELY SUPERCHARGED AND ENERGIZED PRAYERS!

Look at Romans 8:26,27 in *The Amplified Bible,* which gives a clearer understanding of the original Greek:

> So too the [Holy] Spirit comes to our aid and bears us up in our weakness; for we do not know what prayer to offer nor how to offer it worthily as we ought, but the Spirit Himself goes to meet our supplication and pleads in our behalf with unspeakable yearnings and groanings too deep for utterance. And He Who searches the hearts of men knows what is the mind of the [Holy] Spirit [what His intent is], because the Spirit intercedes and pleads [before God] in behalf of the saints according to and in harmony with God's will.

I pray right now that God will give you a fresh revelation of how the Holy Spirit intercedes through you. As you begin to pray, the Holy Spirit will come to your aid. He will reveal to you how you should pray. He takes your petitions and requests and intercedes on your behalf before God, with deep groanings which are too deep for words.

What an awesome picture! You kneel before the Father in prayer. The Holy Spirit is inside of you taking your requests and petitions to the Father and interceding with deep groanings and praying according to God's will. Christ, your great High Priest, stands at the right hand of the Father, making intercession for you. "Wherefore he is able also to save them to the uttermost that come unto God by him, seeing he ever liveth to make intercession from them" (Heb. 7:25).

The Father listens to the groanings of the Spirit, searches the mind of the Spirit and releases the answer to the request you have presented in the name of Jesus! The Father hears the groanings of the Spirit and knows what is in the mind of the Spirit because the Spirit is interceding according to the Father's will.

I like how Andrew Murray described praying in the Spirit: He said it is "The Spirit breathing, the Son's intercession, the Father's will—these three become one in us."

When you know that the Holy Spirit is interceding before the Father, according to His will, on your behalf, there is no doubt that the Father hears you and that whatsoever you ask you will receive!

> And this is the confidence that we have in him, that, if we ask any thing according to his will, he heareth us: and if we know that he hears us, whatsoever we ask, we know that we have the petitions that we desired of him (1 John 5:14,15).

When we pray in the Spirit, we are no longer limited by our natural understanding. Not only does the Holy Spirit reveal to us how to pray, he reveals the things God has prepared for us so that we can *ask*—make a demand on God's promises—and receive what we need and desire from Him.

The apostle Paul said, "I will pray with the spirit, and I will pray with the understanding also" (1 Cor. 14:15). As we pray in the Spirit, our prayers are divinely supercharged and energized. They supersede human limitations! They penetrate into the spirit realm and God's power is released to work and accomplish His will!

I am convinced it will take the Holy Spirit-energized prayers of God's people to demolish Satan's strongholds, shake his kingdom in the nations and open doors that are now closed to the gospel!

We cannot root out and destroy the satanic powers and principalities that have been exerting dominion over cities and nations for hundreds of years with anything less than prayer—prayer that will pierce the darkness.

In our own natural understanding we cannot know or recognize the evil principalities and powers that have established strongholds in our communities, cities or nations. We cannot face these principalities with head knowledge! It takes spiritual discernment through the Holy Spirit to expose evil principalities, and power and authority flowing through us in prayer to demolish their strongholds.

HOLY SPIRIT-ENERGIZED PRAYERS SET DOMINION IN ORDER

The type of prayer we must have today is the same type of prayer that was released through the disciples in the Early Church.

When Peter and John were thrown into prison and later released, what did they do? They prayed! They did not try to determine a strategy to face persecution in their limited understanding. They prayed Holy Spirit-energized prayer that shook the building. "And when they had prayed, the place was shaken" (Acts 4:31).

When Paul and Silas were in prison, what did they do? They prayed and sang praises at midnight and the prison was shaken! (See Acts 16:25,26.) The foundation was broken up. The doors were opened and the chains were broken from them as they prayed.

Recently I was in Mexico City for one of our mobilization meetings for our Mission to All the World Mexico outreach. My associate ministers and the Mission to All the World team for Mexico were with me. We were in a two-story building. As we began to pray we prayed under such an anointing, something happened! The police came running into the building. They said, "You must stop whatever it is you are doing! We've been around the perimeter of this building and the whole building is being shaken!"

They said, "There's an earthquake in this building and you've got to stop it!" We heard what the police were saying but we could not shut it off. We could not stop praying. The chandeliers and the walls started shaking.

Because of the prayers going up, not only did we see a physical manifestation of the building being shaken by God's power, in the spirit realm something was also happening. The kingdom of darkness over Mexico was being shaken by the Holy Spirit-energized prayers of God's people!

The devil's strategy is to try to cause you to use carnal weapons. He wants you to be silent and to pray religiously.

Your mouth is an instrument of authority to cause you to rule and reign in the presence of your enemies. The words coming out of your mouth that are directed and anointed by the Holy Spirit set dominion in order. They enable you to decree into the devil's territory what God has spoken.

When you pray in the Spirit or pray words directed by the Holy Spirit, your words are like mighty swords that enable you to wage war against Satan and his evil principalities. Don't be silent or pray in your mind. There are many conservative people who pray silently. They believe because they have a quiet and reserved personality that they should be very quiet and reserved when they pray.

The prayers that move the hand of God are not dictated by our personality, but by the Spirit of God living within us. We are told to come *boldly* before the throne of God to receive help in our time of need (see Heb. 4:16). Jesus said, "And from the days of John the Baptist until now the kingdom of heaven suffereth violence, and the violent take it by force" (Matt. 11:12).

I have never seen anyone become spiritually violent in prayer by praying silently or conservatively. When we allow the Holy Spirit within us full freedom to pray through us, we are no longer limited by the type of personality or natural disposition we may have, but we pray according to the power of the Spirit within us! We must allow the Holy Spirit to have full expression through us.

> *The Holy Spirit prays through you to execute judgment against the powers of darkness.*

Pray in the Spirit! Pray in unknown tongues! And as you pray, the Holy Spirit prays through you to execute judgment against the powers of darkness and they must go! The work of the enemy will be exposed!

The Holy Spirit will not only reveal the demonic forces that must be bound; He will also reveal the enemy's strategies and give you a divine, foolproof strategy to defeat the enemy!

THE HOLY SPIRIT EXPOSED SATAN'S STRATEGY TO KILL ME

Let me give you a personal example of how the Holy Spirit exposed the strategy of Satan to kill me.

In 1960, I went to Haiti. The Full Gospel Businessmen's Fellowship International was invited by the president of Haiti, and they asked me if I would come and conduct a crusade while they had business meetings.

We rented the biggest stadium in the heart of Port-Au-Prince, which seated 35,000. We had posters up all over the place, and we landed in the middle of the Mardi Gras season.

During Mardi Gras in Haiti, the celebration lasts for seven weeks and for seven Sundays in a row anything goes. Five thousand women have been known to be raped on the streets in one night. Haiti is perhaps the most demonic nation we have in the Western Hemisphere. I would say there is more demon power present there than I have ever seen in Africa or India.

The witch doctors took my picture, stuck pins in it and danced around while my picture went up in smoke. There are more witch doctors in Haiti than any country I have ever seen in my life! Even more than in Africa.

I landed with all of the businessmen at the airport, and a motorcade was waiting. A Spirit-filled Haitian senator by the name of Arthur Bonhomme was there to take us to see the president. We were to ride by the presidential palace where he was waiting on his balcony. As we began the trip, I felt a pain in the pit of my stomach.

I thought I was going to die. I said to the senator, "Would you mind if I don't go by the palace?"

He said, "Oh, the president's waiting."

I said, "Please sir, I'm very sorry, please take me to my hotel."

So they took the car out of the motorcade. I got into my room, fell on the floor like one dead and cried out to God.

I said, "God, what's happening? Am I going to die?"

He said, "No, son, I allowed this to happen to you for a reason. I want to call you aside. I want to talk to you."

Immediately the sickness left me while I was prostrate before the Lord in prayer.

I said, "God, what is it?"

He said, "I want to tell you that tonight when you go into the crusade service, there will be 300 witch doctors there who have made a plan to kill you. They are going to come up against the platform as soon as you start speaking and try to get the people into a mob frenzy. Then they are going to try to come and destroy you and the meeting. They don't like it that you're here in the middle of Mardi Gras."

I said, "Father, I thank you for telling me, but am I supposed to die? If you want me to die, I will die. I will be a martyr."

Then God said to me, "Son, when you go out to that meeting tonight, I want you to know that the word that is in your mouth is My word. Whatever you speak, I will bring to pass."

The meeting was a mess. The witch doctors were shouting and chanting, and the preachers were trying to get control of the meeting. Demos Shakarian, founder and president of the Full Gospel Businessmen's Fellowship International was trying to bring order to the meeting but it was impossible (Demos is now in the presence of the Lord).

I came into the meeting and was asked to speak immediately. I was instantly put into a position of leadership over the gathering because nobody knew what to do. I stood up and greeted the people. I had a Bible school student as my interpreter. I will never forget him. He was a little skinny Creole boy. I shook my finger in his 19-year-old face and said, "Son, you listen to me carefully, now. Whatever word I speak, don't dare misinterpret it. You say exactly what I say."

His knees were shaking as he looked at me because all around us it appeared a riot was about to break out. He probably thought he was surely going to die. I started to try to preach. I opened the Bible and started to read the first six verses from Isaiah 53.

I could not get past the first verse.

They started their chants as they had done during the preliminary time. I tried to read the Word but it was impossible. I called for order. They stopped for about three seconds and started up again. I called for order. They stopped for about three seconds. It went three times like this.

Then I stood up and said with authority, "People of Haiti, I want to tell you something. The true God, the only God, the Living God, has sent me to Haiti. He has sent me here with a message of love and healing for you, but He has shown me that there are many witch doctors here tonight who have come to destroy the meeting."

God showed me exactly how they would dress and how I could identify them. So I started pointing them out and said, "We're going to find out tonight whether or not you have greater power than the power of the God I serve!"

I turned around and looked at all the dignitaries seated on the platform. I said in front of all these dignitaries, "I take no responsibility when the next witch doctor opens his mouth to break up this meeting and they carry him out of this stadium, *dead!*"

The place became quiet. A prophetic mantle fell, and I preached for about 20 minutes. All of a sudden, somebody let out a scream from the back of the stadium where there were 4,000 or 5,000 people standing. (There were 15,000 people in the stadium on this opening night.)

I saw them push a little child over the heads of the people toward the stage.

I said to my interpreter, "What is going on?"

He said, "I don't know, Brother Cerullo, but somebody's shouting, 'I'm healed! I'm healed! I'm healed!' "

"Please get somebody up here to tell me what it's about," I replied.

They finally got the little child up to the front and the mother and father came screaming through that crowd, shouting, "My child is healed! My child is healed!"

It was a little girl, born totally blind, about four years of age, held by her mother. Her eyes popped open, she started to talk to her momma and feel her face and say, "I can see, I can see, I can see!" On the platform, a general stood up with his beautiful military uniform on. I can see him to this day. He put his hands on his head and screamed.

I turned to my interpreter and said, "What's going on?"

He said, "Dr. Cerullo, he is screaming, 'My God, My God, that's my neighbor!'"

That little blind child lived next door to this general, and this healing brought incredible spiritual changes for him and many other Haitians. The crusade went on for three solid weeks, night and day!

Yes, all of this happened to God's glory because He had opened my spiritual eyes and revealed Satan's strategy in advance. While on my knees in my hotel room, even before I walked onto the platform during the crusade, God revealed to me what was needed.

YOU WILL SEE THINGS YOU HAVE NEVER SEEN BEFORE!

I will never forget what God spoke to me that unforgettable night in Haiti: "The word that is in your mouth is My Word. Whatever you speak, I will bring it to pass."

I believe this is the power and authority God is placing in the mouths of His people today so that when we pray or speak under the direction and anointing of the Holy Spirit, it will be done. In this new dimension of power and authority, God will use us to fulfill His will and bring in the end-time harvest.

How does one experience this type of power and authority? How does one speak the words of God and see them come to pass? You may think this power and authority is limited to prophets, pastors or well-known evangelists.

It isn't!

As this end-time prophetic prayer anointing is being released, if you will accept by faith the prophetic word God is releasing and submit yourself fully to the Holy Spirit, He will anoint your mouth. As the Holy Spirit is released in your life in a greater dimension than you have ever experienced, you will pray prayers that will break through the enemy's resistance. Your prayers will be divinely directed and anointed by the Holy Spirit.

One of the greatest keys to praying prayers that will enable you to see God's will fulfilled in your life, in your family, in your city and in your nation is *spiritual vision.*

God has shown me that as this prophetic prayer anointing is released, you will be able to see things in the Spirit you have never seen before. The Holy Spirit will reveal God's prophetic plan and will to you, and as you "see" in the Spirit, you will pray prophetic prayers. God will anoint your words and use your prayers to change the spiritual environment in your personal life, in your home, in your city and nation.

One of the major reasons the Church is not walking in the dimension of power and authority God intended it to experience is because we have not prayed with spiritual vision. The majority of Christians have had a limited awareness of what God wants to accomplish in their lives. They have been unable to see what God is directing them to do, see or say in the Spirit. They are unable to recognize or see the strategies of the enemy or how he is attacking them until they are in the middle of a crisis. As a result, their prayers do not "hit the target" because they have not prayed with spiritual vision.

If you want to be used by God in this end-time hour to accomplish His plan and purposes, to see His will fulfilled in your life and the lives of your loved ones, to see the powers of darkness shaken and your city and nation reached for the kingdom of God, you must pray with spiritual vision.

In the life of Jeremiah, we see a powerful example of what it means to have spiritual vision. Jeremiah was commissioned by

God as a prophetic intercessor. I like to call Jeremiah one of God's specialists. You will find in the near future God will raise up specialists in these last days.

Jeremiah was a specialist who understood strongholds. God trained him in strongholds. God revealed to Jeremiah clearly what He had called and anointed him to do. The Lord touched Jeremiah's mouth and said to him,

> "Now, I have put my words in your mouth. See, today I appoint you over nations and kingdoms to uproot and tear down, to destroy and overthrow, to build and to plant" (Jer. 1:9,10, *NIV*).

God has shown me that as this end-time prophetic prayer anointing is released, there will be many who will receive this same anointing for the ministry God has called them to.

- They will uproot!
- They will pull down!
- They will destroy!
- They will throw down, but they will also build and plant!

Take this prophetic word:

The anointing is coming. God will anoint their mouths and put His words in their mouths to pray prophetic prayers that will root out, pull down and destroy the devil's strongholds. They will also pray prophetic prayers and declarations God gives them for peoples, nations and specific regions of the world.

God will use them to bring about changes that will result in fulfillment of His will in the nations. When they pray or speak, they will know the words coming out of their mouths are not their own because their mouths will be anointed with coals off the altar!

God also gave Jeremiah spiritual vision to see in the Spirit what He was going to do in the nation of Israel. Then, as he spoke the words God put in his mouth, God manifested His power and fulfilled the words coming out of his mouth.

God spoke to Jeremiah and said, "What do you see, Jeremiah?" (Jer. 1:11, *NIV*).

Jeremiah answered, "I see the branch of an almond tree" (v. 11, *NIV*).

The Lord said, "You have seen correctly, for I am watching to see that my word is fulfilled" (v. 12, *NIV*).

A second time God asked Jeremiah, "What do you see?" Jeremiah answered Him, "I see a boiling pot, tilting away from the north" (v. 13, *NIV*). Then God revealed the judgment He was bringing upon the people of Israel because of their idolatry and rebellion against Him. God opened Jeremiah's spiritual eyes and allowed him to see into the future what He was going to do regarding the nation of Israel.

Elisha was a man of spiritual vision. He saw beyond the natural circumstances into the realm of the Spirit. He was not limited by his natural vision.

When Elisha was surrounded by the king of Syria's army with their horses and chariots, he didn't react according to what he saw with his natural eyes but what he saw through his spiritual vision— what the Lord had revealed to him by His Spirit. "When the servant of the man of God got up and went out early the next morning, an army with horses and chariots had surrounded the city. 'Oh, my lord, what shall we do?' the servant asked" (2 Kings 6:15, *NIV*).

Elisha's eyes weren't focused on the city surrounded by the chariots and horses of the king's army, but he saw a greater army, the armies of heaven on horses and chariots of fire. He didn't see defeat, he saw victory! In your circumstances, what do you see? Do you see your overwhelming circumstances or God's provision to meet your needs?

 God wants you to be a man or woman of spiritual vision.

Elisha's servant was overwhelmed with fear because he was only seeing with his natural eyes. Elisha saw something ordinary men could not see. God had given him spiritual vision to see beyond the natural, beyond the circumstances into the supernatural realm of the Spirit! Elisha said to him,

> Fear not: for they that be with us are more than they that be with them. And Elisha prayed, and said, LORD, I pray thee, open his eyes, that he may see. And the LORD opened the eyes of the young man; and he saw: and, behold, the mountain was full of horses and chariots of fire round about Elisha (2 Kings 6:16,17).

WE MUST PRAY WITH SPIRITUAL VISION!

God wants you to be a man or woman of spiritual vision. When you pray, He doesn't want you to pray according to what you see with your natural eyes or understanding or according to your circumstances. He doesn't want you to pray with your eyes focused on your problems; He wants you to pray with your spiritual vision focused on His unlimited power and His promises to you.

When you pray, God doesn't want you to pray with your eyes focused on the power of the enemy but on the power of the Holy Spirit within you to uproot, tear down and destroy every demonic stronghold.

When you pray, God doesn't want you to pray with your eyes focused on any power or ability you possess or the power of your prayers. He wants you to have your spiritual vision focused on the unlimited power of God and the power and authority you have through the Holy Spirit living within you.

How do you develop spiritual vision?

By getting on your face before God. By setting your face like Daniel did to seek God through prayer and fasting. By depending on the Holy Spirit to reveal what God is saying or directing you to do. God gave us the Holy Spirit to reveal Christ to us and to reveal the things that are to come.

Jesus said, "Howbeit when he, the Spirit of truth, is come, he will guide you into all truth: for he shall not speak of himself; but whatsoever he shall hear, that shall he speak: and he will show you things to come" (John 16:13).

That's SPIRITUAL VISION!

God is asking you the same question He asked Jeremiah: "What do you see?"

When you pray for your physical problems—sickness, disease or infirmities—are you praying according to what you see with your natural eyes or according to the spiritual vision God has revealed to you through His promises? As you pray, are the words coming out of your mouth the words He has given you to pray that are anointed and empowered by the Holy Spirit?

When you look at your community and city, what do you see? Do you see neighborhoods torn apart by gang violence, racial strife, and streets filled with prostitutes and people addicted to drugs and alcohol? Or do you have spiritual vision to see

God's purpose and plan for your city?

When you pray do you pray according to the problem or are you praying with spiritual vision? When you pray for your nation, do you pray according to what you see with your natural eyes or with the spiritual vision God has revealed to you? What do you see?

Do you see a nation that has turned its back on God and whose people have turned themselves over to the god of this world? Do you see people who are blinded by Satan and are serving idols and following after the wickedness of their own hearts? Is your spiritual focus on the strength of the enemy? Is your focus on the forces of darkness controlling people that have established strongholds which seem impossible to penetrate?

What has God revealed to you in prayer that He wants to accomplish in your life, in your family, in your city and in your nation? What has God revealed that He is doing in the Spirit to fulfill His prophetic purpose and will in your life and ministry? What do you see?

Has God opened your eyes and given you His spiritual vision, so that you can pray prayers that will be used by God to shake the devil's kingdom and to establish His will? In every circumstance or problem you face, don't act or pray according to what you see with your natural eyes. Pray according to your spiritual vision and what God has already revealed in His promise regarding His will and what He will do for you.

When you pray for your city and nation, don't pray according to what you see in the natural. Don't rely on your natural understanding. Pray in the Spirit—in unknown tongues. Allow the Holy Spirit to flow out of you like a mighty river bursting through a dam.

Pray and ask God to open your eyes and give you spiritual vision to see what He is doing, what His purpose and plan are.

Ask Him to direct your prayers, to anoint your spirit and mouth so that you will pray according to what He has purposed. As God gives you spiritual vision, pray Holy Spirit-energized prayers that will pierce the darkness.

Pray this prayer over your city:

Father,

In the mighty name of Jesus, release your power and anointing to flow over this city. In the name of Jesus, I declare every unlawful work of the enemy to be bound! Spirits of hatred, violence, murder, lust, drug and alcohol addiction, I command you, in the name of Jesus, to loose your hold and leave this city. I tear down your strongholds through the power and authority of almighty God, who lives within me!

Father, release a spirit of conviction and repentance upon the people of this city. Release a spiritual hunger into the hearts of the people.

I declare in Your name that this city belongs to Jesus and that God's Word will be proclaimed in every neighborhood in a demonstration of Your power. I pray that Your Spirit will be poured out in every church and that there will be a great harvest of souls won into Your kingdom!

CHAPTER

7

CHRIST'S SPIRITUAL LEGACY FOR HIS CHURCH

As God releases this last great anointing, an end-time prophetic prayer anointing upon the Church, He is positioning us to overcome every obstacle and win the end-time battle of the ages. The things that will be happening in the remaining years before Christ raptures the Church will be unprecedented.

While the world is thrown into utter chaos and confusion because of the crises that are yet to come, the Church will not be fearful. We will not be confused or perplexed. We will walk under this powerful, end-time prophetic prayer anointing.

In the morning, we will pray. Throughout the day, we will surround all our activities with prayer. In the evening, we will shut ourselves in with the Lord to worship, to intercede, to wage war and to receive His direction. We will live under this heavy prayer anointing.

The Church will come together for corporate prayer sessions. Ministries, churches and prayer groups will unite for strategic prayer for their churches and cities. As the Church comes together in unity through prayer, there will be major advances made both in the spiritual and natural realms that will advance and accelerate the ministry of the Church worldwide.

Doors will open that, in the natural, seem impossible. The Church will move into new, uncharted territory on all levels of society and reach into new arenas with a powerful witness of the gospel.

When the people of the world do not know how to cope with the world's failing systems and deal with the crises they face, God's people will have the answers. They will know what is coming and the action they need to take because God will reveal it to them in prayer. Not only will He reveal things and events that will be taking place and the strategies of the devil; God will reveal strategies for the Church to follow in winning great victories.

As we enter this new dimension of power and authority in prayer, advances will be made that will enable the Church to multiply and increase its outreaches even into the most remote areas of the world. The gospel will penetrate every region of the world and produce a great harvest of souls within every tribe, nation and people group.

As this last great anointing is released, the Church will operate in greater power and authority to produce changes in the Spirit realm. These changes will enable us to impact cities, nations and regions of the world with a greater concentration of evangelism and mobilization for world harvest.

When I refer to this end-time prophetic anointing and the new dimension of power and authority through prayer, I am not talking about just a new concept for prayer or a new methodology. It is much more than that. What I am talking about is an anointing from God that will incorporate every aspect of our lifestyle and will enable us to experience greater victories through prayer in every area of our lives.

God wants prayer to be incorporated into every aspect of our lives. He wants prayer to permeate our homes, our churches, our schools, our neighborhoods, our governments and every area of our environment. And He intends us to release this prayer anointing as we pray for all those we meet who need salvation, healing and deliverance.

God wants to reveal to you and give you a greater understanding of:

- The new dimension of prayer into which He is bringing you;
- New strategic spiritual warfare prayer;
- The position of the Church in prayer;
- What the focus of the prayers of the Church should be in this end-time hour.

OUR SPIRITUAL LEGACY

At the most crucial moment in the history of mankind, Christ prayed a prayer for the Church that has transcended time. It has extended to every age and nationality since Christ lived on the earth 2,000 years ago. In this prayer, Christ prayed for seven major things to be fulfilled in the Church. This powerful prayer is our spiritual legacy. It was one of the last things Christ did before He laid down His life on the cross.

The seven specific things in this prayer, which Christ prayed to be manifested in His Church, are vitally important. As His prayer is fulfilled in your life, you will be prepared and equipped to fulfill all that God has called you to do in this end-time hour.

As we look at these seven important things Christ intends to be manifested in our lives, we must join with Christ and His prayer for His Church and make them the prayers of our hearts.

The spiritual destiny of the world hung in the balance.

The untold agony, shame and disgrace of the cross were before Him. He had gathered His disciples together to share one final moment with them to prepare and strengthen them for what they would soon face.

He was not fearful. He was not worried. He was not trying to determine an alternate plan that would relieve Him from His suffering and death on the cross. There was absolutely no doubt or confusion about what God had called and anointed Him to do. He knew He was returning to the Father and that His disciples were going to face a great onslaught of the enemy.

The prayer He prayed was divinely directed. The words He spoke contained the power for their fulfillment. I believe the moment the Father heard Him, His petition on behalf of His disciples and the Church was granted!

Without a doubt, this is one of the greatest prayers ever prayed! It is sacred. It is timeless. It reveals the very heartbeat of Christ, our great High Priest, His undying love for His Church and what He plans to accomplish in our lives.

The same passion that beat in Christ's heart for His Church in His final moments on earth is what His heart yearns for *now*. And the Holy Spirit is now working within the Church to fulfill and bring to full completion all that He prayed.

CHRIST'S SEVENFOLD PRAYER

In this one prayer, the veil is pulled back from our eyes and we are taken by Christ into the very holy of holies. We are transported into the throne room and are ushered into the sacred presence of almighty God. There, we are given a glimpse of the intimate communion between the Father and the Son as Christ prepares to walk the road to Calvary in fulfillment of His Father's will.

Christ lived in unbroken communion and fellowship with His Father. He lived a life of prayer. Apart from this one great prayer which John recorded, we have only a few portions of Christ's prayers and teachings on prayer recorded. However, it is not just through the form and content of His prayers, but through His example and life of prayer that we can truly learn how to pray effectively as He prayed and experience the same results.

In these final moments together, Christ warned His disciples of the persecution they would soon face and also promised to send the Comforter, the third Person of the Trinity, who would remain with them and would guide them into all truth (see John 16:7-15).

He knew the hour had come when He would face Satan and defeat him. He knew and was ready to suffer the untold agony of the cross, die, and on the third day rise from the dead. He also knew that through His death and resurrection, the Father would be glorified.

What an awesome moment! He took the bread in His hands, signifying His body, which would be broken and offered to God as the ultimate sacrifice to redeem and reconcile men to Himself. He broke the bread, blessed it and gave it to His disciples saying, "Take, eat; this is my body" (Matt. 26:26).

Then He took the cup with the fruit of the vine, representing His blood that would be poured out to cleanse man of his sins and said, "Drink ye all of it; for this is my blood of the new testament, which is shed for many for the remission of sins" (Matt. 26:27,28).

By His own example, He demonstrated how the disciples should have a servant's heart and be willing to serve one another. See our great High Priest as He rises from the table, wraps a towel around His waist, pours water into a basin and begins to wash the disciples' feet (see John 13:4-17).

He gave them a new commandment by which they were to live. He told His disciples, "A new commandment I give unto you, that ye love one another; as I have loved you, that ye also love one another" (John 13:34).

CHRIST'S PRAYER REVEALS HIS HEART FOR HIS CHURCH

Although He faced the greatest battle of the ages when He suffered pain no other man had ever suffered to fulfill God's plan of redemption, His greatest desire was to glorify the Father.

It was a sacred moment as Christ lifted up His eyes toward heaven and began to talk with the Father. "Father, the hour is come; glorify thy Son, that thy Son also may glorify thee" (John 17:1).

A hushed silence fell among the disciples as they focused on every word falling from His lips. What an awesome moment in the history of mankind! In a few moments, He would walk out of the room, where He had spent time alone in intimate fellowship with His disciples, and walk across the Kidron Valley to Gethsemane. In Gethsemane He would be betrayed, forsaken and led away by Roman soldiers to be beaten, mocked, spit upon, tried and sentenced to a cruel death on the Cross.

Christ had finished the work He had been given to do and He asked the Father to restore Him to the glory He had even before the foundation of the world. When Christ came to the earth, He had humbled Himself. Although He was the Son of God, He left His glory in heaven, stripped Himself of His heavenly attributes and took on the form of flesh and blood. Now, as He prepared to return to the Father, He first asked to be restored to His former glory. Christ prayed, "And now, O Father, glorify thou me with thine own self with the glory which I had with thee before the world was" (John 17:5).

At this very strategic moment, when the spiritual destiny of all mankind was in His hands, the major focus of Christ's prayer was neither for Himself nor for strength to face the great battle which lay ahead of Him. His prayer was focused on His disciples and the Church.

Although He came to die for the sins of the world and reconcile sinners to the Father, He did not pray for the world. He did not pray for the sinners or the ungodly. He prayed for all those who would believe in Him. He prayed for you and me.

Every word He spoke to the Father on behalf of His disciples and for the Church is significant and pregnant with divine purpose.

This great high-priestly prayer must not be taken lightly. It reveals Christ's heart and His undying love for His Church, for you and me. He told the Father, "I pray not for the world, but for them which thou hast given me; for they are thine" (John 17:9). He said, "Neither pray I for these alone, but for them also which believe on me through their word" (John 17:20).

In His final hours upon the earth, Christ prayed for you! Let the full significance of His words go deep into your spirit. In that sacred moment, Christ, your great High Priest, prayed for seven specific things to be fulfilled in your life.

1. He prayed the Father will "keep" you.
2. He prayed the Father will sanctify you through His Word.
3. He prayed you will have His joy fulfilled in your life.
4. He prayed the Church will be united together as one with Him and with each other.
5. He prayed the Church will be brought to full maturity. He knew this would have to be the process of an experience and it would not be easy.
6. He prayed God's love will be manifested in you.

7. He prayed you will live in His presence and behold His glory.

JESUS ASKED THE FATHER TO "KEEP" YOU

Think about Christ, our great High Priest, praying for you in this crucial moment of time. He saw through the corridors of time and knew the battles His Church would face. As your High Priest, He knows your weaknesses. He knows the trial and temptations you face. He knows your infirmities and the pain you bear. And He is at the right hand of the Father interceding on your behalf. "For we have not an high priest which cannot be touched with the feeling of our infirmities; but was in all points tempted like as we are, yet without sin" (Heb. 4:15).

Jesus knew His disciples would soon face great turmoil and the onslaught of the enemy. He warned them they would be hated, thrown out of the synagogues and face imprisonment and death. However, He did not ask the Father to remove them out of this dangerous environment or the coming conflict. He asked the Father to *keep* them through the power of His name. He said,

> And now I am no more in the world, but these are in the world, and I come to thee. Holy Father, *keep* through thine own name those whom thou hast given me, that they may be one, as we are (John 17:11, emphasis added). I pray not that thou shouldest take them out of the world, but that thou shouldest *keep* them from the evil (John 17:15, emphasis added).

There are two different Greek words used in this prayer for the word "keep." The word *tereo* means to preserve and *phylasso* means to guard or protect against external attack.

Jesus said, "While I was with them in the world, *I kept them in thy name:* those that thou gavest me *I have kept,* and none of them is lost, but the son of perdition; that the scripture might be fulfilled" (John 17:12, emphasis added).

In essence, Jesus was saying to the Father, I preserved them. I guarded and protected them through the power of Your name. Now that I am leaving, You keep, preserve, guard and protect them by Your name.

YOU ARE PROTECTED BY THE POWER OF HIS NAME!

The name of God Almighty represents all that He is—His power, His grace, His mercy and all His divine attributes. All the power and authority of God Himself resides in His name.

You are being KEPT, preserved, guarded and protected from all evil by the power of almighty God! NOTHING CAN DEFEAT OR DESTROY YOU!

Jesus, in the form of human flesh, manifested God's name to the disciples and to the world. Through His words and actions He revealed God's character and all that His name represents. He was a visible representation of all that God's name means.

He told the Father, "I have manifested thy name unto the men which thou gavest me out of the world" (John 17:6). "I made Your Name known to them and revealed Your character and Your very Self, and I will continue to make [You] known" (John 17:26, *AMP.*).

God is all powerful. He is all knowing. He is the mighty Creator. He spoke the universe into existence. There is no greater power in heaven or in earth. This is the power that is behind His name!

In His prayer Christ asked the Father to keep, preserve, guard and protect us from all the powers of the evil one through the unlimited power of His name! Do you realize what this means to you?

In answer to Christ's prayer, you are being *kept*, preserved, guarded and protected from all evil by the power of almighty God! *Nothing can defeat or destroy you!*

Christ did not pray and ask the Father to remove you from difficult circumstances, trials or temptations. He did not ask that you would never have to face the power of the enemy. He did not ask the Father to remove you from the evil, ungodly society in which we live. He placed you where you are and gave you a mission to fulfill.

Regardless of what you may face, there is absolutely nothing that can defeat or destroy you. You can face any fiery attack of Satan: persecution, disaster or personal tragedy, knowing God will *keep* you. Every trace of doubt or fear will disappear and you will live your life in total confidence when you know that you are being kept by the power of almighty God.

The apostle Paul was persecuted, stoned, beaten, shipwrecked and imprisoned. At one point in his life, his closest friends deserted him. But he never wavered in his faith. He had total confidence that God would not only deliver him out of the hand of the enemy but also would keep, preserve and protect him. Listen to his confession of faith: "And the Lord shall deliver me from every evil work, and will preserve me unto his heavenly kingdom" (2 Tim. 4:18).

Knowing that the Father heard and has answered Christ's prayer, claim this promise by faith. Face every problem, every circumstance, every weakness, every temptation and every attack of the enemy with absolute confidence, knowing He will *keep* you!

Receive the answer to Christ's prayer and apply it today in your life. Every morning when you wake up, praise the Father that He is keeping you. Tell Him,

> *Father,*
>
> *I receive the prayer of Your Son over my life. Thank You for keeping, preserving, guarding and protecting me from all evil. I know that You will protect me from every attack of the enemy and You will deliver me. I will be victorious in every trial, every test and every battle I may face!*

CHRIST PRAYED FOR HIS CHURCH TO BE SANCTIFIED!

The second thing Christ asked the Father to do for us was to "sanctify" us. He prayed: "Sanctify them through thy truth: thy word is truth. As thou hast sent me into the world, even so have I also sent them into the world. And for their sakes I sanctify myself, that they also might be sanctified through the truth" (John 17:17-19).

Think about the eternal significance of this prayer. In the final hours before He was to lay down His life on the cross, Christ lifted His eyes toward heaven and cried out to the Father, "Sanctify them!"

The word "sanctify" means to consecrate or set apart, to dedicate for holy service to God. Jesus said, "And for their sakes I sanctify myself" (v. 19). He was sinless, pure and undefiled by sin or the world. "For such an high priest became us, who is holy, harmless, undefiled, separate from sinners, and made higher than the heavens" (Heb. 7:26). His sanctification was that He was setting Himself apart, consecrating and dedicating Himself to fulfill the divine purpose of God by laying down His life as a holy sacrifice for man's sin.

In His intimate intercession with the Father on our behalf, Christ asked Him to sanctify us, to set us apart from the world. Jesus said concerning His disciples, "They are not of the world, even as I am not of the world" (John 17:16).

Those who truly belong to Christ and are part of His Church have separated themselves from the world. The apostle John wrote, "Love not the world, neither the things that are in the world. If any man love the world, the love of the Father is not in him" (1 John 2:15).

The call of the Spirit is clear: "Come out from among them, and be ye separate;...touch not the unclean thing; and I will...be a Father unto you, and ye shall be my sons and daughters" (2 Cor. 6:17,18).

Do not be deceived. Christ is coming for a pure, chaste Bride that is holy and wholly set apart for Him. Christ gave Himself for the Church, "That he might present it to himself a glorious church, not having spot, or wrinkle, or any such thing; but that it should be holy and without blemish" (Eph. 5:27).

FULLY DEDICATE TO THE FULFILLMENT OF GOD'S DIVINE PURPOSES

Christ interceded for us. He said, "Sanctify them!" The work of sanctification can only be accomplished in our lives as we submit ourselves to the Holy Spirit.

Sanctification is a supernatural manifestation of a holy, righteous God in the lives of those who are willing to fully yield themselves to Him. It is a process that takes place only as we are willing to set ourselves apart from the world and dedicate ourselves wholly, as Christ did, to the fulfillment of God's divine purposes.

We no longer belong to the world. We are the chosen, sanctified, set apart Church of the living God! We are no longer our own and we must no longer live our lives to please ourselves. We have been bought with a great price and we now belong wholly to Christ. We are servants of the great King of kings and Lord of lords! We have been marked by God, chosen, set apart and anointed by His Spirit to fulfill His divine purposes.

IT IS TIME FOR GOD'S PEOPLE TO CRY OUT, "SANCTIFY US!"

Jesus is coming soon! As we prepare ourselves for His coming, we must focus on this important factor of Christ's intercession for us. We must lift our voices and cry out to God, "Sanctify us!" The Word declares, "Follow...holiness, without which no man shall see the Lord" (Heb. 12:14). "Sanctify yourselves therefore, and be ye holy: for I am the Lord your God" (Lev. 20:7).

The time has come for God's people to practice what we preach! One of the reasons the Church is not walking in the dimension of power God intended is because we have compromised with the world and allowed sin to remain in our lives. How can we expect God's power to flow through us unhindered when we are not living holy, sanctified lives set apart unto God?

The Holy Spirit will flow through you only in proportion to the extent you allow God to sanctify and cleanse you. God will not release His power to flow through unclean vessels. As long as there is unconfessed sin in your life, you will not be able to pray effectively.

In His prayer, Christ reveals *how* we are sanctified. He prayed, "Sanctify them through thy truth: thy word is truth" (John 17:17). Christ knew we could not attain holiness through our own efforts. It is a supernatural work of the Holy Spirit. That is why He asked the Father to sanctify us through the truth and then said, "thy word is truth."

Beloved, we are sanctified, set apart from the world, cleansed and made holy through the truth, the Word of God. Christ sanctifies and cleanses us by the "washing of water by the word, that he might present [us] to himself a glorious church, not having spot, or wrinkle" (Eph. 5:26,27).

Knowledge of the Word is not enough. You can know the truth of the Word but it will not change you until it is applied to your life. We are sanctified as we know the truth of the Word, submit ourselves to the Holy Spirit and walk in obedience to it! This can only be accomplished through the power of the Holy Spirit working within us.

Do you really want to be used by God? Do you want His unlimited power flowing through you to meet the desperate needs of the world?

It is very significant that in the final hours of His life Christ prayed for His Church that we should be sanctified, cleansed, made holy and set apart to fulfill His divine purposes. If He placed this much importance upon our need to be sanctified, we must also make it our utmost desire. We must earnestly pray and ask God to sanctify and make us holy as He is holy.

Make Christ's prayer yours. Cry out to the Father:

Lord,

> *Sanctify me through Thy truth; Thy Word is truth. I hunger after You. Holy Father, make me holy as You are holy. Cleanse me with Your Word. I fully submit myself to You and consecrate myself wholly to do Your will. Reveal everything in my life that is displeasing to You and purge it out of my life.*

CHRIST PRAYED FOR YOU TO HAVE HIS JOY IN FULL MEASURE!

The third thing Jesus prayed is that *His joy* would be fulfilled in our lives. Jesus told the Father, "I am coming to you now, but I say these things while I am still in the world, so that they may have the full measure of my joy within them" (John 17:13, *NIV*).

Christ's purpose for your life is that you will have the *full measure of His joy!*

Christ knew that after He returned to the Father, His disciples and all who professed His name would be thrown into a sea of great turmoil. He knew they would be persecuted, beaten, imprisoned, thrown to the lions and martyred for the sake of the gospel.

As He sat and ate with them on their last evening together, He warned them that they would be hated, thrown out of synagogues and killed. He knew their hearts were filled with sorrow because He was leaving them. He had told them that they would weep and lament as a woman in travail. But He also promised them, "Your sorrow shall be turned into joy" (John 16:20).

Yes, Jesus knew their hearts were already overwhelmed with sorrow. He had told them, "And ye now therefore have sorrow: but I will see you again, and your heart shall rejoice, and *your joy no man taketh from you*" (John 16:22, emphasis added).

In essence, Jesus was saying, "You may be overcome by sorrow now, but just wait! I will see you again. On the third day, when I come up out of the grave, something's going to happen to you! You're going to have joy greater than anything you have ever known. You will have *My joy* that cannot be destroyed! It's going to be *full measure!* It's going to be deep inside your being, and nothing, no power on earth, no evil principality, nothing will be able to take it from you!"

HIS JOY WILL SUSTAIN YOU IN YOUR DARKEST HOUR!
Christ, knowing what His disciples faced, prayed they would have His joy in *full measure* because He knew it would sustain them in their darkest hour. Christ also looked down through the corridor of time and saw what we would face in this end-time hour.

He knows the sorrows, heartaches, trials and testing you have gone through. He has seen the struggles, the pain and the hours you have cried in despair. He has seen the battles you have faced. But He has planned for you to have His joy deep inside your being that will sustain you regardless of the battles, trials or circumstances you may face.

 Christ prayed that you will have His joy in full measure so that you can rejoice in your darkest hour of pain and sorrow.

"The joy of the Lord is your strength!" (Neh. 8:10). One of Satan's greatest weapons against the Church today is a spirit of discouragement. He knows that if he can cause you to get your eyes on your problems, your sickness, your financial problems, or problems in your family relationships instead of focusing on God's promises and His love for you, you will become discouraged.

God has shown me there are many Christians who have become so discouraged they have lost all hope. Their faith has become weakened and they have lost their joy. As a result, they are ready to give up.

No one can take Christ's joy from you. But you can lose it. And if you allow him to, Satan will take it from you.

In the circumstances you are facing right now, do you have His joy flooding your soul? Christ wants you to have His joy in *full measure* so that you can rejoice even in your darkest hour of pain and sorrow. His joy is a supernatural joy that comes from His Spirit living within you. It is not a joy that the world can give. It is a joy that only He can give. It is a joy that will make you sing and rejoice even when it seems as if everything around you is crumbling. His joy will enable you to walk in victory over every obstacle you will face.

Christ knew you would need His joy in *full measure* to overcome every fiery dart of the enemy and endure every trial in 100 percent victory.

Make this your prayer:

Dear Lord,

> *Fill me now with Your joy. Teach me to rejoice and praise You in every circumstance that I face. In Jesus' name, I break every spirit of discouragement from my life. By faith, I receive Your joy in full measure. Let it flow out of the depths of my innermost being. Your joy is my strength! Amen.*

CHRIST PRAYED FOR THE UNITY OF THE CHURCH

The fourth thing that Christ prayed for was that His Church would be united together as *one.* Hear the cry of His heart:

> That they all may be one; as thou, Father, art in me, and I in thee, that they also may *be one in us:* that the world may believe that thou hast sent me. And the glory which thou gavest me I have given them; that they may be one, even as we are one (John 17:21,22, emphasis added).

In those final, crucial moments with His disciples, He prayed for His Church to be vitally united together as *one.* Christ knew

what they would face: fiery trials, persecution and death for the
sake of the gospel. He knew they would face the onslaught of the
enemy in an attempt to crush and totally destroy the Church.

Christ also looked down through the corridor of time and
saw the inner struggles His Church would face throughout the
ages that would weaken and dilute its power. Knowing the battles
we would face, He prayed for the one ingredient that would
make the Church a powerful, indestructible force capable of not
only withstanding every attack of the enemy, but of taking the
world for the kingdom of God—UNITY!

Christ not only prayed for every member of His Church to be
vitally united together as one with each other, but that we also
be united as *one* with Him and with the Father.

CHRIST'S PRAYER WILL BE FULFILLED!

Let His heartbeat ring in your ears: "That they all may be
one...that they also may be one in us" (John 17:21), and "that
they may be one, even as we are one" (v. 22).

Christ prayed for unity that would be such a dynamic, dom-
inant force in the Church that it would be a living witness to the
world that He was sent by God and was who He claimed to be. It
is not a man-made, superficial unity. This type of unity will
never be produced through men's striving to attain it or through
their futile attempts to bring all churches and denominations
together under one structure. We will always have differences in
doctrine and methods of worship and church administration.
Such unity that Christ prayed for the Church cannot be produced
by natural means or methods, but by the divine flow of His
Spirit living within us!

In 1989 when God revealed to me five major waves of the
Holy Spirit coming to the Church in the decade of the nineties,
He showed me a major wave of *unity of the spirit.*

Beloved, as His Spirit is being poured out on the Church, one of the true manifestations of His Spirit will be one of love and unity drawing members of the Body, ministries and churches of all denominations together as *one in the spirit*!

Regardless of what we see outwardly, unity in the Spirit is coming to the Church. There is no doubt Christ's prayer for His Church will be fulfilled!

CHRIST PAID THE PRICE FOR UNITY
WITH HIS OWN BLOOD

Not only did Christ pray for the members of the Church to be united as *one*, He paid the price for our unity with His own blood. Through His death on the cross, He not only paid for our salvation, He made it possible through the indwelling of His Spirit that every member be united together in *one body*. The apostle Paul told the Corinthians,

> For by one Spirit are we all baptized into one body, whether we be Jews or Gentiles, whether we be bond or free; and have been all made to drink into one Spirit (1 Cor. 12:13).

Paul told the Ephesians,

> There is one body, and one Spirit, even as ye are called in one hope of your calling; one Lord, one faith, one baptism, one God and Father of all, who is above all, and through all, and in you all (Eph. 4:4-6).

Christ not only prayed for His Church to be divinely united together with Him as *one body*, He poured out His blood, making it possible! Through His sacrifice on the cross, every true born-again believer has been "made to drink into one Spirit" (1 Cor. 12:13).

And it is that *same* Spirit within every true believer that draws us together and unites us as one body. Regardless of the unique distinctions, characteristics and differences with the Church of Jesus Christ today, there is only *one* Body, *one* Spirit, *one* Lord, *one* faith, *one* God and Father! True born-again believers have all been redeemed by the blood of Jesus, called by His Spirit and made *one* with Him.

UNITY COMES THROUGH A DIVINE
FLOW OF GOD'S SPIRIT

Unity in the Spirit is manifested within the Church as the Spirit draws us together into a vital relationship with Christ and with one another.

The key to true unity in the Spirit is your relationship with Christ. As you yield fully to the Holy Spirit and are vitally united as *one* with Christ, the Spirit will conform you into His image. His life will flow out of you! By His Spirit working within you, there will be a divine flow of His love drawing and uniting you together with other members of the Body of Christ.

The Spirit of God that unites you as one with Christ will break down every barrier and destroy every dividing factor keeping you from walking in unity with other members within the Body of Christ. But you must be fully yielded to the Holy Spirit.

The apostle Paul told the believers in Philippi, "Stand fast in one spirit, with one mind striving together for the faith of the Gospel" (Phil. 1:27). He told the believers in Galatia, "Make every effort to keep the unity of the Spirit through the bond of peace" (Eph. 4:3, *NIV*).

CHURCH UNITY IS THE KEY TO A FULL
MANIFESTATION OF GOD'S POWER AND GLORY.

I must confess, there have been many times when I have looked at the division, strife, jealousies and barriers between pastors, churches and various denominations and wondered if Christ's prayer for unity in the Church would ever be fulfilled.

Last year, during a Mission to All the World mobilization meeting in Brazil, God showed me how the Church can be united in the Spirit. God told me, "Show them My heartbeat." I asked Him, "What is Your heartbeat?" He answered, "Souls!" At that moment, I realized that the place where the Church can truly be united is in our love for God and for the lost!

Unity in the Spirit within the Body of Christ is the key to a full manifestation of God's power and glory within the Church in this crucial end-time hour. It is the key to the fulfillment of the Mission to All the World mandate God gave us. We must be willing to lay aside our differences and unite together as one mighty force to reach the world with the gospel before Christ returns.

Make the passionate cry of Christ's prayer your own. Cry out to the Lord:

Lord,

> *Make me truly one with You and one with all true believers who are part of Your Body. I yield myself completely to the Holy Spirit. Remove everything that keeps me from walking in unity. Release a divine flow of Your love through me and use me as an instrument to bring healing, forgiveness and unity to the Body of Christ.*

United prayer is the seed that will produce a harvest of souls. The Body of Christ must unite through intensified prayer, weeping and travailing together, as never before, on behalf of the lost in our cities and nations. It is our united prayers that will activate God's power and enable us to reap the end-time harvest of souls.

CHRIST PRAYED FOR YOU TO BE MADE "PERFECT"!

The fifth thing that Christ prayed would be manifested in His Church is that we will be brought to full maturity where we are a full manifestation of Christ to the world.

Jesus prayed, "I in them, and thou in me, that they may be made perfect in one" (John 17:23). The Greek word for "perfect" means to be brought to full maturity.

By His Spirit, members of the Body of Christ are all joined together in one body. Paul told the Corinthians, "For by one Spirit are we all baptized into one body, whether we be Jews or Gentiles, whether we be bond or free; and have been all made to drink into one Spirit" (1 Cor. 12:13).

Every born-again believer is joined by God's Spirit to Christ, who is the "Head" of the Church. God's purpose is that members of the Body of Christ grow together in unity until we reach full spiritual maturity, where we have been incorporated and joined together into *one* "perfect man."

Before Christ ascended into heaven, He placed the fivefold ministry in the Church to bring us to a position of "perfection" whereby we are doing the work of the ministry and building up the Body of Christ. Paul said the fivefold ministry was given,

> For the perfecting of the saints, for the work of the ministry, for the edifying of the body of Christ: till we all come in the unity of the faith, and of the knowledge of the Son of God, unto a perfect man, unto the measure of the stature of the fullness of Christ (Eph. 4:12,13).

Beloved, do you realize the significance of what this means to you?

Satan's objective is to keep us in a position of spiritual ignorance where we cannot see or understand God's plan and purpose. He does not want the Church to reach the full stature of Jesus Christ because he knows he is defeated and fears what will happen when the Church takes its position as full-grown sons of God!

IT IS TIME FOR THE CHURCH TO REACH FULL MATURITY!

Before the foundation of the world, according to the good pleasure of His will, God planned for the adoption of children through Jesus Christ (see Eph. 1:3-6). He desired to have a people through whom He would manifest His power and glory to the world.

God planned for you to be conformed and changed into the image of Christ. "For whom he did foreknow, he also did predestinate to be conformed to the image of His Son, that he might be the firstborn among many brethren" (Rom. 8:29).

The "perfection" Paul was referring to is the position of maturity we reach when we have come to full age, where we stand, full grown. This full maturity is nothing less than Christ's own perfection.

Through Christ's supreme sacrifice, He has already fulfilled everything necessary to make it possible for you to be perfected and to reach the full stature of Jesus Christ.

This is not something that is a remote possibility, or something that can be achieved through your own personal efforts. However, you can know that it will happen because as Christ was preparing to return to the Father, He prayed, "I in them, and thou in me, that they may be made perfect in one" (John 17:23).

Christ's prayer for His Church will be answered!

Not only has God made full provision for you to be brought to full maturity, He has placed His life—the Holy Spirit—within you to bring you to this position where you have grown to the full stature of Jesus Christ.

The life and the power to bring you to full maturity is in the "seed" of the Father that is in you. The life, nature and characteristics of the Father are in that seed. You have been born again by an incorruptible seed, and it is through that seed Christ's life will be manifested in your life.

Growing up into the full stature of Jesus Christ is the result of the continuous work of the Holy Spirit, and as you continually surrender and yield yourself to Him, His seed remains in you, producing His life and causing you to grow into Christ's stature.

Paul said we are to grow "unto a perfect man, unto the measure of the stature of the fullness of Christ" (Eph. 4:13). The word "fullness" is translated from the Greek word *pleroma*, which denotes fullness, that of which a thing is full. In this verse it is used to refer to all Christ's virtues and attributes!

In Christ dwells all the "fullness" of the Godhead. "For it pleased [the Father] that all the divine fullness (the sum total of the divine perfection, powers and attributes) should dwell in Him permanently" (Col. 1:19, *AMP.*).

Christ prayed, "I in them, and thou in me, that they may be made perfect in one" (John 17:23).

The key to reaching the full stature of Jesus Christ is your union with Him. In Christ, you are filled with the fullness of the Godhead and reach full spiritual stature where you are a full manifestation of Christ to the world.

Christ intends His Church to be a full manifestation of His mind, His vision, His will, His anointing, His consecration, His power and authority, His faith, His wisdom, His righteousness, His love and all that He is!

The key to reaching this position of full maturity is your union with Christ. You must remain in Him where there is a continual flow of His life in and through you to the world.

Make Christ's prayer your desire:

Lord,

> *Make me one with You. Draw me into a new dimension and higher level of prayer where I am in continual fellowship with You. I desire You above all else. I yield myself fully to Your Spirit. Conform me into Your image. Change me...remove every sin, every hindrance, and form Your life in me.*
>
> *Give me Your mind, Your wisdom, Your vision, Your will, Your faith, Your power and authority, Your righteousness, Your love. Let Your life flow through me in a full manifestation of Your power and glory to the world.*

As God brings the Church in the end-time hour into this position of full maturity and we stand in the full stature of Christ, we will see greater breakthroughs than we have ever experienced. God's power and glory will flow out of us as a mighty end-time witness that Christ is the Son of the living God.

CHRIST PRAYED GOD'S LOVE WOULD BE MANIFESTED THROUGH THE CHURCH

The sixth thing that Christ prayed to be manifested in the Church was God's love. How we need a fresh manifestation of God's love in the Church today! We must have it to bring us into true unity where we will be able to reach the world with the gospel before Jesus returns!

There in the Upper Room on His last evening with His disciples, He emphasized these seven important, key truths that He wanted them to remember and put deep into their spirits.

Time after time, He emphasized the importance of loving one another. Jesus told the disciples:

- A new commandment I give unto you, That ye love one another, as I have loved you, that ye also love one another. By this shall all men know that ye are my disciples, if ye have love one to another (John 13:34,35).
- This is my commandment, That ye love one another, as I have loved you. Greater love hath no man than this, that a man lay down his life for his friends (John 15:12,13).
- These things I command you, that ye love one another (John 15:17).

Jesus knew that when He was gone, the disciples would face such intense persecution and such an onslaught of the enemy to destroy the Church that they needed a supernatural manifestation of God's love to be able to overcome the power of the enemy. He knew they needed God's love flowing through them to unite them together as a mighty force to spread the gospel to the ends of the earth.

Jesus prayed, "O righteous Father, the world hath not known thee: but I have known thee, and these have known that thou hast sent me. And I have declared unto them thy name, and will declare it: *that the love wherewith thou hast loved me may be in them, and I in them*" (John 17:25,26, emphasis added).

The type of love Christ prayed to be manifested in the Church was not a natural love. It was a supernatural love. It is the same love that the Father had for Christ. The disciples were to love one another as Christ had loved them. This supernatural love was to be the distinguishing factor, setting each of them apart from the world as one of His disciples.

Jesus didn't tell them that the world would recognize them

because of the power that was manifested or the miracles they performed. He told them that people would know and recognize them as His disciples by the love that was manifested by them one to another. He said, "By this shall all men know that ye are my disciples, if ye have love one to another" (John 13:35).

The type of love our Father manifested to us that made Him willing to send His only begotten Son to the world, to be beaten, mocked, spit upon and crucified on our behalf is the type of love Christ prayed would be in us. "Behold, what manner of love the Father hath bestowed upon us, that we should be called the sons of God" (1 John 3:1).

The type of love Christ prayed would be manifested in the Church is the same love that He demonstrated for us that made Him willing to lay down His life and endure the agony, shame and disgrace on the cross. He told His disciples, "Greater love hath no man than this, that a man lay down his life for his friends" (John 15:13).

God's love was a powerful energizing force in the lives of the disciples and believers in the Early Church. It was the major key to the power of God that was manifested through them. They had so much love they were willing to lay down their lives for one another. They were so filled with love for God, they were willing to be thrown to the lions, thrown into prison, beaten, tortured and burned at the stake. It was God's love burning within them that united them together as a mighty, united force that could not be defeated. They operated in the power and authority of God because they walked in love.

They did not merely say they loved one another. They demonstrated it! Their love for one another was a demonstration of the reality of the gospel and a witness to the world that Christ was who He claimed to be. There was no earthly power that could quench that love.

Now, let me ask you some questions. Do you see this same manifestation of God's love flowing in the Church today? Do you love your brothers and sisters in the Lord with the same love Christ has for you? Do you love other members of the Body of Christ enough to die for them?

WE MUST HAVE A FRESH BAPTISM OF GOD'S LOVE!

Beloved, when we take the mask off, we cannot say that this same dimension of God's love is being manifested in the Church. It is sad to say, but true, that as our churches have grown in size, in many instances they have also become cold and impersonal.

Within a great majority of our churches, the people do not even know one another. They have not made time to build relationships. In many churches there is jealousy, bitterness, resentment, unforgiveness and hatred among the members. There is a spirit of competition, jealousy and bitterness among ministers of the gospel.

In some cities, there is more of a demonstration of love coming from the people of the world than from the Church. If the Church does not have this type of love for one another that Christ demonstrated, how will we ever be able to reach the millions of unsaved people we have never seen?

John wrote, "If a man say, I love God, and hateth his brother, he is a liar: for he that loveth not his brother whom he hath seen, how can he love God whom he hath not seen?" (1 John 4:20).

If we truly have God's love in our lives, there will be a true manifestation of it through us to one another. What we need in the Church today is more than the surface, phony words coming out of our mouths.

I don't know about you, but if someone tells me they love me, I want them to prove it. Not to just say it, but to demonstrate it through their actions. John wrote, "My little children, let us not love in word, neither in tongue; but in deed and in truth" (1 John 3:18).

I have often told my family and staff, "Don't wait until I am in a grave before you send me flowers. Give me roses while I am living!" If all we do is tell our brothers and sisters we love them and fail to show it through our actions, it isn't truly God's love. God demonstrated His great love by sending us His most valued and treasured possession—His only Son.

Christ demonstrated His unsurpassing love by giving His life by dying on the cross. We need a fresh revelation of God's love and the love we must have for one another! In the Church we need to demonstrate God's love flowing through us by helping one another. When we see a brother or sister in need, we need to minister to their needs.

Our prayers must be fueled by God's love; otherwise, they are just empty words and we are only going through the motions.

If you see a brother or sister who needs new clothes, go buy them some clothes. If you see a brother who needs a car and you have two cars, give him one of yours. If you see a sister who is a single parent struggling to make ends meet to care for her children, do what you can to help her. John wrote, "But whoso hath this world's good, and seeth his brother have need, and shutteth up his bowels of compassion from him, how dwelleth the love of God in him?" (1 John 3:17).

How can we pray effectively, "with all perseverance and supplication for all saints" (Eph. 6:18), unless we truly have God's love burning in our hearts for one another? Our prayers must be fueled by God's love; otherwise, they are just empty words and we are only going through the motions. Jesus said, "And when ye stand praying, forgive, if ye have aught against any: that your Father also which is in heaven may forgive you your trespasses. But if ye do not forgive, neither will your Father which is in heaven forgive your trespasses" (Mark 11:25,26).

We can only pray fervently when our prayers are motivated and fueled by God's love. If there is anger, unforgiveness, bitterness or resentment in our hearts toward others, our prayers will not be heard. Beloved, the Church needs a fresh baptism of God's love!

When Christ prayed for the Church that we would have the same love for one another that He has for us, He knew we would need it to fulfill the Great Commission and bring in a great end-time harvest of souls. We need to pray for God to baptize and saturate us with His love so that we will manifest that love to one another and so the world will have a demonstration of God's love as a witness that Christ is alive and He is the mighty resurrected Son of God!

Make this prayer the cry of your heart:

Father,

I want to be a channel of Your love. Reveal the depth of Your love to me and baptize me now with Your love. Cause it to flow out of me to my brothers and sisters in the Body of Christ. Help me to demonstrate Your love through my actions. Reveal any hatred, bitterness or unforgiveness and remove it from my heart.

Help me to manifest Your love in ministering to the needs of others, by lifting their heavy loads. Remove all selfishness and

give me Your servant's heart so that I will be able to love my
brothers and sisters as You have loved me.

CHRIST INTENDS HIS CHURCH TO BE A FULL MANIFESTATION OF HIS GLORY!

The seventh thing Christ prayed for His Church is that we will live in His presence and behold His glory. As He began His prayer He said, "Father, the hour is come; glorify thy Son, that thy Son also may glorify thee" (John 17:1). Jesus knew the hour had come when He would return to the Father and He asked the Father to restore the glory He had with Him before the foundation of the world (see v. 5).

The word "glory" is translated from the Greek word *doxa* which refers to all that God has and all that He is. It is referring to all His divine attributes. When Jesus came to earth, He laid aside the glory He had with the Father and took on the form of man. Although He was God in the flesh, He laid aside His divine attributes.

While He was on earth He was a reflection of God's glory. The glory of God shone forth and was manifested in both Jesus' character and the things He did. God's power and glory were revealed as He healed the sick, proclaimed the words of life, cast out devils and raised the dead. He revealed His glory through the love, mercy, forgiveness, joy, peace, authority and power He demonstrated. Paul described Jesus as "being the brightness of his glory, and the express image of his person" (Heb. 1:3). As Christ was a visible manifestation of God to men on earth, He intends you to be a visible representation and reflection of His glory to the world.

Because of His obedience even unto death, God exalted Christ and restored to Him the glory He had before He came to earth. He is in a highly exalted position. In this glorified position He now possesses all the divine attributes He laid down before He came to earth. Christ intends His glory to be reflected through you. In His prayer for the Church, He told the Father, "And the glory which thou gavest me I have given them; that they may be one, even as we are one" (John 17:22).

Through His Spirit living within us, He has given us His glory. God's purpose through Jesus' death and resurrection was to bring many sons into glory (see Heb. 2:9,10). He planned to bring you into a relationship as a true son whereby the glory of Christ, who dwells within you, will be reflected in an outward expression to the world.

God has planned for you to be conformed into the image of Christ. "For whom he did foreknow, he also did predestinate to be conformed into the image of his Son" (Rom. 8:29). As you yield to the Spirit working within you, you are being changed, transformed "into the same image from glory to glory, even as by the Spirit of the Lord" (2 Cor. 3:18). Your body is a vessel, a channel through which the glory of God can be manifested to the world because of Christ living in you!

Christ also prayed that we would live with Him and behold His glory. He said, "Father, I will that they also, whom thou hast given me, be with me where I am; that they may behold my glory" (John 17:24).

Christ intends for His Church to be a full manifestation of His glory to the world in this end-time hour! The world will see His glory as His power and anointing are released through our lives in this powerful new dimension of prayer, in healing the sick, casting out demons and proclaiming the gospel!

We also have the promise that when He appears, we will appear with Him in glory. Paul said, "When Christ, who is our life, shall appear, then shall ye also appear with him in glory" (Col. 3:4).

Beloved, we will see Him as He is in all His power and glory and *we will be like Him!* "But we know that, when he shall appear, we shall be like him; for we shall see him as he is" (1 John 3:2).

All that Jesus prayed in this great prayer for His Church will be fulfilled! Do not take this prayer lightly. Christ gave you this prayer as your spiritual legacy. Receive it and act on it. Each of the seven things He included in this prayer He intends to be manifested in your life.

In this end-time hour before He returns, He has planned for His Church to grow to full maturity where we are a full manifestation of His power and glory—all that He has and is—to the world.

1. Pray and believe God to keep, preserve, guard and protect you through the power of His name!
2. Pray and ask God to sanctify, cleanse and set you apart from the world through His Word!
3. Pray and believe God to release His joy into your life in full measure!
4. Pray for the unity in the Spirit to be manifested in the Church!
5. Pray and ask God to bring you to full maturity, by His Spirit working within you until you are a full manifestation of Christ to the world.
6. Pray for God to baptize you with His love and that it will be manifested through you to your brothers and sisters in the Body of Christ!
7. Pray for Christ's power and glory to be manifested through you to the world!

CHAPTER
8

THE SPIRIT AND THE BRIDE
SAY, "COME!"

Something supernatural is now taking place within the Church that is preparing us for Christ's coming. God is breathing deep into our spirits something so unique, so powerful, unlike anything any other generation has ever experienced.

As this last great anointing is released, God is planting within us a deep longing and hunger after Christ, to know Him in all His fullness, to see Him in all His glory, to be molded into His likeness. Christ's prayer for His Church is being fulfilled.

There is an all-consuming passion and a spiritual intensity growing within us for Christ to return and receive us to Himself. There is a longing to behold Him and to live in His presence.

Are you longing to see the Lord? The cry of David's heart was, "As for me, I will behold thy face in righteousness: I shall be satisfied, when I awake, with thy likeness" (Ps. 17:15). Nothing else on this earth will ever fully satisfy the longing in our hearts until we behold Christ in all His glory and see Him face-to-face!

The Early Church lived with a continual sense of expectancy

concerning Christ's return. However, in these closing moments of time, the intensity and desire of the end-time Church for Christ to return is far greater and will continue to increase until there is a united cry ascending to heaven. No other generation has experienced this bridal cry of the Church for the bridegroom.

The Spirit of God is stirring within us, saying, *I am preparing you...the consummation of the ages is here.* The manifestation of what we have lived for is upon us. It is calling us.

There is a fixed time in God's timetable that He has planned for Christ's return. It is an unalterable fact. Once the prophesied end-time events begin, they will happen rapidly in succession. *Nothing* will prevent them.

Jesus said no one knows the day or the hour when He will return, not even the angels or Christ Himself! But He said when we see the end-time signs being fulfilled, we can know for a certainty that He is at the door, on the threshold of heaven, and the angel has the trumpet of God to his mouth and is ready to signal Christ's return.

One of the major signs Jesus said must happen before He returns is that the gospel must first be preached in every nation. He said, "And this gospel of the kingdom shall be preached in all the world for a witness unto all nations; and then shall the end come" (Matt. 24:14).

Christ's return is inseparably linked to the completion of the Great Commission. And the key to its fulfillment is the united prayer of the Church. The key to its fulfillment is the Church rising up with this end-time prophetic prayer anointing.

OUR PRAYER MUST BE, "COME, LORD JESUS!"

We are now witnessing an unprecedented move of the Spirit, calling the Body of Christ to prayer. I believe this global call to prayer is the key to the fulfillment of the Great Commission, which will signal the time for Christ's return.

Only through intensified, united prayer and fasting will we be able to gather in the greatest end-time harvest of souls this world has ever seen. "They that sow in tears shall reap in joy. He that goeth forth and weepeth, bearing precious seed, shall doubtless come again with rejoicing, bringing his sheaves with him" (Ps. 126:5,6).

Our prayers on behalf of the lost will enable us to reap the end-time harvest. The Word is the seed, but our prayers are what will water the seed to produce the harvest!

Daniel said, "And I set my face unto the Lord God, to seek by prayer and supplications, with fasting, and sackcloth, and ashes" (Dan. 9:3). He cried out to God, confessing the sins of the people, "O Lord, hear; O Lord, forgive; O Lord, hearken and do; defer not, for thine own sake, O my God: for thy city and thy people are called by thy name" (v. 19).

God has given us a revelation of the lateness of the hour. Like Daniel, we must set our faces and go before God in seasons of prayer and fasting. We must confess our sins, the sins of our churches, cities and nations. We must pray for a revival of repentance and restoration. It is time for God's people to sound the alarm and get on their faces before God in prayer! The eleventh hour is upon us and we must not fail to stand in the gap for the multiplied millions of unreached people who have not yet heard the gospel.

The cry of our hearts must be, "Come, Lord Jesus!"

Before Christ comes, a mighty cry must rise up and cover the earth. The prayer upon the lips of every born-again believer must be, "Come, Lord Jesus!" Deep from within the innermost recesses of our spirits, there must be a cry, a yearning after and longing for His return.

My spirit is so stirred! And yet, I do not believe there is even 1 percent of Christians in the Church today who are praying for our Lord's return. Beloved, when was the last time you prayed for Christ to return?

I am convinced that we will have to pray King Jesus back! Christ will return *in answer to the prayers of His Church!*

THE TRUMPET OF GOD IS ABOUT TO SOUND!

Beloved, I pray that Christ will reveal to you the lateness of the hour. I believe His coming is sooner than we think.

In Revelation chapter 22, three times Jesus said, "Behold, I come quickly."

In verse 7 He said, "Behold, I come quickly: blessed is he that keepeth the sayings of the prophecy of this book." In verse 12 He again says, "And behold, I come quickly; and my reward is with me, to give every man according as his work shall be." He says His last words to the Church in verse 20, "Surely I come quickly."

Our response to Christ must be, "Come quickly, Lord Jesus!"

In Revelation 22 verse 17 we read, "And the Spirit and bride say, Come."

Listen carefully.

When the true Bride of Christ comes into full agreement with the Spirit and into the fullness of the Spirit in this end-time hour, together we will cry out to Christ, *Come!*

And He will come as the Father releases Him to take His bride unto Himself!

WATCH AND PRAY!

When Jesus taught His disciples concerning His coming, He gave them a very sobering command. He said:

> Watch ye therefore: for ye know not when the master of
> the house cometh, at even, or at midnight, or at the
> cockcrowing, or in the morning: lest coming suddenly
> he find you sleeping. And what I say unto you I say unto
> all, Watch (Mark 13:35-37).

He told them:

> Watch ye therefore, and pray always, that ye may be
> accounted worthy to escape all these things that shall come
> to pass, and to stand before the Son of man (Luke 21:36).

God has revealed to us what is coming to the earth; He has
revealed the lateness of the hour; and He is now directing the
Body of Christ to watch in prayer. Jesus said, "Watch ye therefore,
and pray always" (v. 36).

It is not something optional He is asking us to do. He
requires it of us. And those who fail to hear and obey what the
Spirit of God is saying to His Church today will not be able to
stand. They will be taken off guard. They will reap heartache and
defeat.

The Greek word used in these verses for "watch" is *agrupneo*
which means not only keeping awake, but looking for and
expecting something to happen. Today, we have a responsibility
before God to be spiritually awake, alert and receptive to what
the Spirit of God is saying. Knowing we are living in the final
hour before Christ's coming, we must be constantly awake, looking
and expecting Him to return at any moment.

A FINAL SEPARATION IS COMING!

A day is soon coming when Christ will issue the command to His
angels to gather His elect together from the four corners of the

earth (see Matt. 24:31). The chaff will be separated from the wheat. The Elect, His end-time remnant, will be caught up to meet Him in the air, and then the door will be closed.

When that final separation is made, there will be Christians saying to the Lord, "We have sat in Your presence. We have heard the Word preached. We have sat at your table and tasted of Your goodness. Lord, open unto us!"

But the door will be forever shut, and they will be thrown into the outer darkness where there is weeping and gnashing of teeth (see Luke 13:25-28).

Christ will reward those Christians who are watching, who are prepared and faithful in doing His will when He returns. He will put them in charge of all His possessions. Jesus said:

> *Therefore keep watch,* because you do not know on what day your Lord will come. But understand this: If the owner of the house had known at what time of night the thief was coming, he would have kept watch and would not have let his house be broken into. So you also must be ready, because the Son of Man will come at an hour when you do not expect him (Matt. 24:42-44, *NIV,* emphasis added).

Jesus then asked the question:

> Who then is the faithful and wise servant, whom the master has put in charge of the servants in his household to give them their food at the proper time? It will be good for that servant whose master finds him doing so when he returns. I tell you the truth, he will put him in charge of all his possessions (Matt. 24:45-47, *NIV*).

The faithful servant is the one who is watching with a constant state of readiness and expectancy. He is the one who is busy not just hearing and talking, but *doing the will of God* regardless of the hour that He comes.

The only way to remain in this state of readiness is through prayer!

A WAVE OF TRUE HOLINESS IS COMING TO THE CHURCH!

Do not be deceived. Jesus is coming for a pure Bride—an end-time holy remnant that is without spot or blemish.

To be prepared you must be watching in prayer. You must stay in a state of spiritual readiness where you are clothed in garments of His holiness and righteousness.

Peter wrote, "Wherefore, beloved, seeing that ye look for such things, *be diligent* that ye may be found of him in peace, without spot, and blameless" (2 Pet. 3:14, emphasis added). When Christ comes there will be a final separation. He will separate the chaff from the wheat, and not everyone who cries, "Lord, Lord" will enter into heaven (see Matt. 7:21).

We must be diligent, prepared, and busy fulfilling the will of God and guarding ourselves from anything that will hinder us from walking in holiness before Him.

One of the five waves of the Holy Spirit God revealed to me that will come in this decade of the Holy Spirit is *a wave of true holiness!* A spirit of true holiness, righteousness and consecration on a new level is coming to the Body of Christ to prepare us for His coming. There will be no more compromise or hypocrisy. Emotionalism will be replaced by serious dedication.

Many Christians today, when they think of a great move of the Spirit, think of an outward manifestation. They associate an outpouring of His Spirit with people shouting, being "slain in the Spirit" and singing and dancing in the Spirit. All of these manifestations are good. However, this coming wave of true holiness goes much deeper—beyond emotionalism.

It will be a deep inner working where Christ will do some deep cleaning in our lives to prepare us for His coming. Christians who

> *We cannot expect to move into this new, powerful, higher dimension of prayer that will shake the devil's kingdom and demolish his strongholds in the nations if we are not living a holy, consecrated life before God.*

are only looking for the outward manifestations—the power and glory—instead of looking to the Lord and asking Him to purge the sin from their lives will not even recognize this great move of the Spirit when it comes.

During this wave of the Holy Spirit, a spirit of righteousness will come upon God's people who want to walk in true holiness. As it comes upon us, it will replace mere emotionalism with a serious dedication and consecration.

GOD IS CALLING THE CHURCH TO A NEW DEDICATION AND CONSECRATION

This last great anointing God is releasing will bring us into a new dimension of power and authority in prayer, and calls for a new dedication and consecration before God.

We cannot expect to move into this new, powerful, higher dimension of prayer that will shake the devil's kingdom in the nations and demolish his strongholds if we are not living holy consecrated lives before God. As long as we allow sin to remain in our lives, it leaves an opening for Satan to attack us.

When the children of Israel went to battle, God fought for them. No one could stand before them. They were invincible! However, when there was sin in the camp they were delivered into the hands of their enemies and lost the battle. Their army went up against the enemy thinking God would give them victory as He had before.

But in the battle against Ai, the children of Israel were defeated. The men of Ai were few in number but they easily routed 3,000 men in Israel's army. Then the hearts of the people were seized with fear because they were powerless before their enemies. Joshua tore his clothes and prostrated himself on the ground before the Ark of the Lord until the sun went down. Listen to his prayer:

> Ah, Sovereign Lord, why did you ever bring this people across the Jordan to deliver us into the hands of the Amorites to destroy us? If only we had been content to stay on the other side of the Jordan! O Lord, what can I say, now that Israel has been routed by its enemies? The Canaanites and the other people of the country will hear about this and they will surround us and wipe out our name from the earth. What then will you do for your own great name? (Josh. 7:7-9, *NIV*).

Defeated, discouraged, ashamed and fearful is how the Israelites felt. Joshua did not acknowledge the possibility that they were unable to stand against the enemy because of some sin or failure on their part. He blamed God.

One of the most difficult things for people to do is recognize and take responsibility for their own sins, weaknesses and failures. They want to shift the blame to someone else—their pastor, their mates, or their children. When they are unable to stand against the attack of the enemy, they often blame God.

The Lord saw Joshua, heard his prayer and commanded him to get up. "Stand up! What are you doing down on your face?" (v. 10, *NIV*). In other words, God was asking Joshua, *Why are you crying out to Me?*

God makes clear the reason the children of Israel had been defeated. He told Joshua:

> Israel has sinned; they have violated my covenant, which I commanded them to keep. They have taken some of the devoted things; they have stolen, they have lied, they have put them with their own possessions. That is why the Israelites cannot stand against their enemies; they turn their backs and run because they have been made liable to destruction. I will not be with you anymore unless you destroy whatever among you is devoted to destruction (Josh. 7:11,12, *NIV*).

The Israelites opened themselves up to defeat because of their sin. God told Joshua to consecrate the people. He told Joshua to tell the people that they would be unable to stand against their enemies until they dealt with their sin.

TO PRAY WITH POWER, WE MUST HAVE PURE HEARTS
If God allowed His chosen people to be defeated before their enemies because of their sins and disobedience, do you think God will enable the Church today to be victorious over the power of the enemy when we allow sin to remain among us?

No! He will not!

We serve a God who is altogether holy. And He expects us to be holy, pure and blameless. God said, "Be ye holy; for I am holy" (1 Pet. 1:16). Paul said, "Follow peace with all men, and holiness, without which no man shall see the Lord" (Heb. 12:14).

As this end-time prophetic prayer anointing is released, we must come before God in prayer lifting up holy hands or we will be defeated! Paul wrote to Timothy, "I will therefore that men pray every where, lifting up holy hands, without wrath and doubting" (1 Tim. 2:8).

If the Church in this end-time hour is going to have power in prayer to tear down Satan's strongholds and take dominion over his power in our homes, cities and nations, we must come before God with holy hands!

The time has come when we must take an honest look at ourselves and allow God to reveal the sin we have allowed to remain in the Church. We need to stop making excuses and rationalizing for our sins and get them under His blood! We need to stop hiding sin or pretending it's not there, and expose all sin to the truth. Pastors and ministers need to stop coddling it and deal with sin as sin!

There is sin in the camp! It is time that we deal with it!

Within the Church we have allowed compromise to gain a major stronghold. We are compromising the Word to fit in with the world's standards! Within the leadership of our churches, there are pastors and ministers who are involved in illicit affairs. They think they have their sin covered. It is not! God sees it, and unless there is repentance, there will be defeat!

Within the Church there are men and women who are bound by lust and who are involved in adulterous relationships yet see nothing wrong with it. They believe they can continue illicit relationships and still be Christians.

There are "Christian" businessmen who think nothing of lying or cheating on their income taxes, who cheat their customers, who purposely misrepresent the facts and who become involved in questionable business deals with unbelievers.

There are Christians who allow their hearts to be filled with all sorts of evil imaginations and fantasies. They want R-rated movies, filled with foul language, sex and violence. They tell dirty jokes on the job, read cheap romance novels and watch the "soaps" on television.

In many churches today worldliness is no longer condemned. It is encouraged through doctrines that are preached causing Christians to set their affections on the things of the world, and teaching them to seek after material possessions.

There are men and women filling our churches today who outwardly appear to be righteous, who have a form of godliness, but are filled with hatred, bitterness, unforgiveness, pride, greed, jealousy and other ungodly attitudes. Is it any wonder that the Church has not taken our cities and nations for the kingdom of God?

God intends the Church to be *invincible* and that none of our enemies will be able to stand before us. He intends there to be no obstacle too great—whether governments, religious strongholds or ideologies, lack of financial resources, lack of natural resources or demonic forces—that we cannot overcome through prayer.

However, like the children of Israel, instead of the enemy running from us, we have been unable to stand and take the victory Christ has already won for us because we have allowed sin to remain in our midst.

Sin separates us from God.

GOD IS TELLING US TO GET RID OF SIN
God is calling us to humble ourselves before Him. He is calling us to confess and turn away from our sins.

Beloved, hear me. Whenever there is unconfessed sin in our lives and we are walking in disobedience to God, He will not hear us. David said, "If I regard iniquity in my heart, the Lord will not hear me" (Ps. 66:18).

If you want to pray with power and authority and see God's promises fulfilled in your life, you must live in accordance with the Word of God. You must have the Word of God deep in your heart so that it takes root and produces changes in your life.

> *The prayers that God hears and answers are prayers that are prayed from a pure heart with pure motives.*

Jesus said, "If ye abide in me, and my words abide in you, ye shall ask what ye will, and it shall be done unto you" (John 15:7). Only as you walk in accordance with the Word will you live in the powerful dimension where you ask anything of the Father in Jesus' name and it will be done. The Lord spoke through Isaiah to the children of Israel:

> BEHOLD, the Lord's hand is not shortened, that it cannot save; neither his ear heavy, that it cannot hear: But your iniquities have separated between you and your God, and your sins have hid his face from you, that he will not hear (Isa. 59:1,2).

The prayers that God hears and answers are prayed from a pure heart with pure motives. It is the fervent prayers of the righteous that God hears, and that produce power. "The Lord is far from the wicked: but he heareth the prayer of the righteous" (Prov. 15:29). The apostle James wrote:

> And the prayer [that is] of faith will save him who is sick, and the Lord will restore him; and if he has committed sins, he will be forgiven. Confess to one another therefore your faults (your slips, your false steps, your offenses, your sins) and pray [also] for one another, that you may be healed and restored [to a spiritual tone of mind and heart]. The earnest (heartfelt, continued) prayer of a righteous man makes a tremendous power available [dynamic in its working] (Jas. 5:15,16, *AMP.*).

If you want to pray prayers with power that will shake the forces of Satan's kingdom, you must be willing to acknowledge your sins, offenses, wrong attitudes, unforgiveness, anger, jealousy and any other sin in your life. Confess it and get it under the blood of Jesus.

In this end-time hour, those who really want to be used by God and desire to live and walk under God's anointing will humbly and circumspectly walk before Him. They will be sensitive to the Holy Spirit and walk in the fear of the Lord. They will guard their hearts and minds from allowing unholy attitudes, unholy thoughts or carnal desires to take root. They will guard the words coming out of their mouths so that they will not sin through backbiting, spreading gossip or speaking evil of others.

They will walk in a new awareness of God's presence and will be careful not to say or do anything that will grieve or quench the Holy Spirit. As they walk in close communion with the Lord, they will be responsive to His voice and His corrections and quick to repent of any sin.

YOU MUST COME TO YOUR OWN ALTAR OF REPENTANCE

God is calling us to a higher level of dedication, consecration and holiness. He is bringing us to a new level of spiritual maturity, and with this new spiritual maturity must come greater accountability and responsibility before God.

Before we can stand in a position of power and dominion with Christ to pray anointed, Holy Spirit energized prayers on behalf of our families, cities and nations, we must first come to our own altar of repentance before the Lord.

When Jesus taught His disciples concerning prayer, He taught them the importance of coming before God in humility and not with a self-righteous attitude. He told a parable about two men who went into the Temple to pray. One was a self-righteous Pharisee and the other a publican. Listen to the Pharisee's self-righteous prayer: "God, I thank thee, that I am not as other men are, extortioners, unjust, adulterers, or even as this publican. I fast twice in the week, I give tithes of all that I possess" (Luke 18:11,12).

The self-righteous Pharisee was caught up in his own self-righteous works. He did not acknowledge his need or dependence upon God. There are Christians today who pray with a self-righteous spirit. They come before God thinking He will hear them because of who they are or because of the works they have done. They do not acknowledge their need or confess their sin. They are already justified in their own eyes.

God will not hear prayers that are prayed from a self-righteous spirit. God resists the proud. "God sets Himself against the proud and haughty, but gives grace [continually] to the lowly" (Jas. 4:6, *AMP.*).

In Jesus' parable, the Publican stood humbly before God. He smote his breast and cried, "God be merciful to me a sinner" (Luke 18:13). He humbly acknowledged his need of God and cried out for mercy. God heard the publican and he went away justified, unlike the self-righteous Pharisee.

God has promised, "If my people, which are called by my name, shall humble themselves, and pray, and seek my face, and turn from their wicked ways; then will I hear from heaven, and will forgive their sin, and will heal their land" (2 Chron. 7:14).

> *Hear the call of the Spirit and humble yourself before God at your personal altar of repentance.*

God wants to do a new work in your life. He wants to bring you into this dynamic, new dimension of prayer where the words coming out of your mouth are used by Him to uproot, tear down and demolish strongholds in your life, in your family, your city and your nation.

Do you want to receive this end-time, prophetic prayer anointing?

Hear the call of the Spirit and humble yourself before Him. Go before God at your personal altar of repentance. Ask God to reveal to you the sins in your life. Cry out to God as David did. "Search me, O God, and know my heart: try me, and know my thoughts: and see if there be any wicked way in me, and lead me in the way everlasting" (Ps. 139:23,24).

Allow God to purge and cleanse you of everything in your life that is displeasing to Him. Ask Him to reveal any wrong attitudes of your heart or strongholds in your mind that need to be changed. If you have hatred, unforgiveness or resentment toward anyone, go to them. Confess it and ask their forgiveness.

Do not allow any opening for the enemy to gain an entrance into your life to weaken you or hinder your prayers.

As the Church is cleansed and God's people walk in holiness and purity before the Lord, their mouths will be sanctified. When they pray, the words coming out of their mouths will be mighty arrows piercing the darkness and destroying the strongholds of Satan. God will direct their words and their prayers to accomplish His will and establish His Kingdom among the nations.

IT IS TIME TO PRAY FOR A DOWNPOUR OF THE FORMER AND LATTER RAIN

One of the key prayers I believe God is directing the Church to pray in these final hours before Christ returns is for God to send the latter rain. God promised: "Ask ye of the Lord rain in the time of the latter rain" (Zech. 10:1).

We are living in a time of harvest when God is bringing to fulfillment the things He has planned for this hour. It is a time when He is bringing His Church into a new position of power and authority! The "former rain" is the rain that softens and prepares the parched ground so that the winter grain may be sown. The "latter rain" is the rain that falls and causes the fruit to ripen for the harvest.

We have had the "former rain" of the outpouring of the Holy Spirit. Now is the season for the "former and latter rain" of the Spirit to fall! Joel prophesied:

> Be glad then, ye children of Zion, and rejoice in the Lord your God: for he hath given you the former rain moderately, and he will cause to come down for you the rain, the former rain, and the latter rain in the first month (Joel 2:23).

It is time to rejoice!

God tells us to *ask* and make a demand on what He has provided! *Ask* for the rain of the Holy Spirit in your life! God will open the heavens and cause a deluge of the former and latter rain of the Holy Spirit simultaneously to be poured out that will be so great it will hasten the ripening of the harvest!

This great end-time outpouring will come quickly and will accelerate the work God has given us of reaching the world with the gospel! Joel prophesied:

> And it shall come to pass afterward, that I will pour out my spirit upon all flesh; and your sons and your daughters shall prophesy, your old men shall dream dreams, your young men shall see visions: and also upon the servants and upon the handmaids in those days will I pour out my spirit (Joel 2:28,29).

Beloved, now is the time for the Church to unite and begin to pray for a *downpour* of the former and latter rain of the Holy Spirit. We must have this last great anointing to enable us to bring in the end-time harvest in the nations.

My prayer is, "Let it pour!"

As the heavens open and the Holy Spirit begins to rain down upon us and we become saturated and drenched with His Spirit, we will walk in the fullness of His power to bring in the greatest harvest this earth has ever seen.

As the Holy Spirit is poured out, those who yield themselves fully to the Holy Spirit will walk under this heavy end-time prophetic prayer anointing. We will come into a new dimension of power and authority in our prayers that will enable us to take the victories Christ has already won for us in the nations.

As we pray Holy Spirit-energized prayers under this end-time prophetic prayer anointing:

- We will see Satan's kingdom shaken by God's power. Bondages will be broken. Strongholds in the nations will be torn down. Evil principalities and powers of darkness now exercising dominion over people groups will be cast out, opening the door for the penetration of the gospel.
- We will take hold of the promises of God and see greater answers to prayer than we have ever experienced.
- We will pray with new revelation and wisdom.
- We will pray bold, prophetic prayers and pray prophetic declarations over our families, cities and nations.
- We will pray apostolic prayers that will change the spiritual destiny of nations.
- We will decree into being the things God has ordered for this end-time hour.
- We will see God's glory manifested in the nations.
- We will pray divinely energized prayers that will bring in the end-time harvest of souls.

Are you hungry for the rain of the Holy Spirit? Are you ready to receive this end-time prophetic prayer anointing? Are you ready to make a new dedication and consecration of your life to God? Do you want to enter a new dimension of power and authority in your prayers? Pray this prayer right now:

Father,
I have heard the call of Your Spirit and I receive the prophetic Word that You have given me. I am ready to receive this end-time prophetic prayer anointing. Anoint my mouth with fire from

Your altar and release a new power and authority in my prayers.

I make a new dedication and consecration of my life and all that I am and all that I have. I humble myself before You and ask You to search my heart. Reveal any sin I have allowed to remain in my life. I come to You with a contrite heart. Forgive me for these sins and cleanse me from all unrighteousness.

Cleanse my heart of any wrong attitudes. Cleanse my mind and release Your Spirit within me so that I will be able to bring every thought into submission to You.

My spirit cries out for the outpouring of Your Holy Spirit. Rain on me! Pour out Your Spirit upon me until I am completely submerged in Your Spirit. Anoint my mouth that I will pray with power and authority the words that are directed by Your Spirit.

Anoint my eyes so that I will have spiritual vision and pray according to what You have revealed to me. Help me keep my spiritual vision focused upon You and Your promises, instead of my problems and circumstances.

Use me to pray bold, prophetic prayers to tear down Satan's strongholds in my life, in my family, in my city and in my nation. I receive from You now the fulfillment of all the promises and prophetic words You have given me.

In Jesus' name, I receive this end-time prophetic prayer anointing!

I will rise up now in the newness of Your strength to fulfill my calling for my end-time destiny!

Maranatha—Lord Jesus come quickly!

And I saw heaven opened, and behold a white horse; and he that sat upon him was called Faithful and True, and in righteousness he doth judge and make war. His eyes were as a flame of fire, and on his head were many crowns; and he had a name written, that no man knew, but he himself. And he was clothed with a vesture dipped in blood: and his name is called The Word of God. And the armies which were in heaven followed him upon white horses, clothed in fine linen, white and clean. And out of his mouth goeth a sharp sword, that with it he should smite the nations: and he shall rule them with a rod of iron: and he treadeth the winepress of the fierceness and wrath of Almighty God. And he hath on his vesture and on his thigh a name written, KING OF KINGS, AND LORD OF LORDS (Rev. 19:11-16).

GLOBAL PRAYER STRIKE FORCE

GLOBAL PRAYER COVERING

When God gave me the mandate to reach the entire world by the end of the year 2000, I knew that one man and one organization could not do it alone. God gave me the key. He told me, *Raise up a prayer covering over the world.*

I am convinced that it will take a mighty army of intercessors, prayer ministries and prayer cell groups worldwide, all uniting to see the fulfillment of the work God has given us to do and bring in the final great end-time harvest of souls.

Our goal is to recruit 10 million intercessors worldwide, as members of the Global Prayer Strike Force. These intercessors will help raise up a prayer covering over the world, to pray for the Lord's return, pray for Mission to All the World and the unreached souls within each of the 10 major world regions.

To date, we have a network of approximately 300,000 intercessors worldwide, along with 239 International Global Prayer Strike Force leaders in 46 countries. Our goal is to establish 1 million Prayer Command Centers worldwide in homes, schools and businesses, which will meet on a weekly basis to pray.

Global Prayer Strike Force teams are trained and mobilized to travel to the MTAW outreaches to pray strategic warfare prayer within each region.

God has raised up major prayer ministries and networks around the world to cover the nations with prayer. Our goal is to link with these prayer networks for MTAW and help fulfill God's mandate of raising up a prayer covering over the world. Here are some of the outstanding ministers and leaders of major prayer networks we are linking with for Mission to All the World 2000:

Dr. C. Peter Wagner and Doris Wagner
Founders, Global Harvest Ministries
P. O. Box 63060, Colorado Springs, CO 80962-3060
(719) 262-9922

Headquartered in the World Prayer Center under the direction of C. Peter Wagner, Global Harvest Ministries is a primary source and catalyst of intercessory prayer for worldwide evangelism.

The goal of Global Harvest is to mobilize as many as 160 million people from all denominations to pray for the unsaved, especially those within the 10/40 Window countries.

Chuck Pierce
Executive Director, the World Prayer Center
11005 State Highway 83, Colorado Springs, CO 80921
(719) 536-9100

The World Prayer Center is a division of Global Harvest Ministries. Their goal is to develop 120 National Prayer Networks and 5,000 local church prayer rooms by the year 2000. Wagner points out:

> The generation in which we live is the first generation in all of human history that has had the potential of fulfilling the Great Commission. Mission to All the World is an

amazing vision. It's not just Brother Cerullo's. It is what the Spirit is saying to the churches. I admonish you. If you're a pastor, missionary, a believer or a church leader, do whatever you possibly can to join this effort to see this gospel preached in all the world as a witness.

Ted Haggard
Senior Pastor, New Life Church
11025 State Highway 83, Colorado Springs, CO 80921
(719) 594-6602

Ted Haggard is the senior pastor of New Life Church in Colorado Springs, Colorado. In 1984, God gave him a vision to plant a church in Colorado Springs. Today he has a thriving church of 3,000 members who are deeply committed to prayer. God also gave him the vision of the World Prayer Center. Ted Haggard and Peter Wagner are cofounders of the World Prayer Center.

Beverly Pegues
Executive Director, the Christian Information Network
11005 State Highway 83, Ste. 159, Colorado Springs, CO
80921
(719) 522-1040

The Christian Information Network is also a ministry of New Life Church. This network coordinates prayer initiatives for believers around the world to pray fervently for the nations in the 10/40 Window.

Believers from more than 105 nations have united to pray for the 10/40 Window. In 1993 they sponsored the prayer initiative Praying Through the Window, and 21 million believers world-wide participated! In 1995 during Praying Through the Window II—millions of believers continued to stand in the gap for the lost in the 10/40 Window.

Here's what Pastor Ted Haggard has to say regarding networking with Dr. Cerullo for Mission to All the World:

Our church, since its very inception, has been sold on missions. We look for opportunities to be involved with missions. That's why we are involved with Mission to All the World 2000. We're excited about Mission to All the World 2000 because it gives us an opportunity to do much more than we could ever do on our own. This is a wonderful opportunity everyone of us has, as churches and individual Christians, to participate with Morris Cerullo, and those who are associated with him, to communicate the gospel, literally, to the whole world. It's our goal that by the end of the year 2000, every single person on planet earth hears the life-giving message of the Lord Jesus Christ.

Cindy Jacobs
President, Generals of Intercession
P. O. Box 49788, Colorado Springs, CO 80949
(719) 535-0977

Cindy Jacobs, president of Generals of Intercession, is an outstanding leader in the area of prophetic intercession for the nations. Her ministry is dedicated to fulfilling their goal of seeing that every unreached people group of the world is receiving strategic prayer by the year 2000 in order to reach them for the gospel.

Dick Eastman
International President, Every Home for Christ
7899 Lexington Drive, Ste. 101, Colorado Springs, CO 80920
(719) 260-8888

Dick Eastman is the international president of Every Home for Christ (formerly World Literature Crusade), a worldwide ministry of house-to-house evangelism that has been working actively since 1946 with more than 400 mission agencies and denominations to place a printed message of the gospel (one for adults and one for children) in every home in the whole world.

Because many areas of the world are virtually closed to all missionary outreach, particularly in Muslim countries as well as the remaining Communist nations such as China and North Korea, Every Home for Christ has developed an especially strong prayer mobilization effort through its multihour Change the World School of Prayer originated by Dick Eastman. More than 1 million Christians in 120 nations have been impacted by this substantive challenge to pray for world evangelization. Eastman says,

> We're involved in a strategy to take the gospel of Jesus Christ, literally, to every home on earth. But it can't be done without the cooperation of ministries working together and training nationals to take the good news to people who have never heard. That is why I'm excited about Mission to All the World 2000. I want to encourage you to participate in this great thrust. Pray for it and give to it. Because, together, we're going to mobilize these people and they will finish the task and reach all the world for Jesus.

Gerald Coates
Pioneer Team
Waverly Abbey House
Waverly Lane, Farmham, Surrey GU9 8EP
ENGLAND
Phone: 01252-784774

This is one of the outstanding Christian prayer ministries God has mobilized worldwide that is stimulating prayer and intercession in over 180 nations of the world. On Saturday, June 10, A.D. 2000 (Jesus Day), up to 20 million will take to the streets to declare that the third millennium belongs to Jesus.